THE

RULES

OF

LIFE

PEARSON

At Pearson, we believe in learning – all kinds of learning for all kinds of people. Whether it's at home, in the classroom or in the workplace, learning is the key to improving our life chances.

That's why we're working with leading authors to bring you the latest thinking and best practices, so you can get better at the things that are important to you. You can learn on the page or on the move, and with content that's always crafted to help you understand quickly and apply what you've learned.

If you want to upgrade your personal skills or accelerate your career, become a more effective leader or more powerful communicator, discover new opportunities or simply find more inspiration, we can help you make progress in your work and life.

Pearson is the world's leading learning company. Our portfolio includes the Financial Times and our education business, Pearson International.

Every day our work helps learning flourish, and wherever learning flourishes, so do people.

To learn more, please visit us at **www.pearson.com/uk**

THE
RULES
OF
LIFE

A personal code for living
a better, happier, more
successful kind of life

RICHARD TEMPLAR

PEARSON

Harlow, England • London • New York • Boston • San Francisco • Toronto • Sydney
Auckland • Singapore • Hong Kong • Tokyo • Seoul • Taipei • New Delhi
Cape Town • São Paulo • Mexico City • Madrid • Amsterdam • Munich • Paris • Milan

PEARSON EDUCATION LIMITED
Edinburgh Gate
Harlow CM20 2JE
Tel: +44 (0)1279 623623
Fax: +44 (0)1279 431059
Website: www.pearson.com/uk

First published 2006 (print)
Second edition published 2011 (print and electronic)
Third edition published 2012 (print)
This edition published 2015 (print and electronic)

© Richard Templar 2006 (print)
© Richard Templar and Pearson Education Limited 2011 (print and electronic),
2012 (print)
© Richard Templar 2015 (print and electronic)

Pearson Education is not responsible for the content of third-party internet sites.

ISBN: 978-1-292-08560-9 (print)
      978-1-292-08562-3 (PDF)
      978-1-292-08564-7 (ePub)
      978-1-292-08561-6 (eText)

British Library Cataloguing-in-Publication Data
A catalogue record for the print edition is available from the British Library

Library of Congress Cataloging-in-Publication Data
A catalog record for the print edition is available from the Library of Congress

10 9 8 7 6 5 4 3 2 1
19 18 17 16 15

Cover design by Nick Redeyoff

Print edition typeset in 10.5/12pt ITC Berkeley Oldstyle Std by 71
Print edition printed and bound in Great Britain by Clays Ltd, Bungay, Suffolk

NOTE THAT ANY PAGE CROSS REFERENCES REFER TO THE PRINT EDITION

This book is dedicated to Miyamoto Musashi, who taught me the strategy of simplicity.

No fear.
No surprise.
No hesitation.
No doubt.

Contents

Partnership Rules 118

Social Rules 180

The Rules of happiness 222

Introduction

For reasons that are too long and complicated to go into here, I had to live with my grandparents for a couple of years when I was very young. They, like many of their generation, were hard-working, contented sort of people. My grandfather had taken early retirement owing to an industrial accident (a lorry-load of bricks fell on his foot) and my grandmother worked in a large department store in London. Having me dumped unexpectedly on her for a while obviously caused logistical problems. I was too young for school and my grandfather wasn't to be trusted to look after me at home (men didn't look after children in those days . . . my, how things have changed). Her solution was to tuck me under her wing – on some days physically as well as metaphorically, as she smuggled me past managers and supervisors – and we went to work together.

Now going to work with 'Nan' was fun. I was expected to keep quiet and still for long periods and, as I didn't know any different, assumed this was normal. I found that by watching customers – often from my safe refuge under a huge desk – I could pass the time quite happily. Thus was born an immense appetite for people-watching.

My mother – later I went back to live with her – said it wouldn't ever get me anywhere. I'm not so sure. You see, early in my career, observation of those around showed that there was a distinct set of behaviours that got people promoted. If there were two people of equal ability, for example, and one dressed, thought and behaved as if they had already been promoted, they would be the one who got the next available job at that next level. Putting these behaviours into practice gave me a fast track up the career ladder. These 'rules' formed the basis of my book *The Rules of Work,* now a bestseller in its field.

Just as you can identify behaviours that make some people glide effortlessly onwards and upwards at work, so you can in life. Observing life in general, people very broadly seem to fall into two main camps: those who seem to have mastered the knack of successful living and those who still find it all a bit of a struggle. And when I say successfully mastered it, I don't mean by amassing wealth or being at the top in some stressful career. No, I mean mastered it in the old-fashioned sense that my hard-working grandparents would have understood. People who are content, mostly happy on a day-to-day basis and in general healthy and getting more out of life. Those who are still struggling tend to be not so happy on the whole, and the enjoyment of life just isn't what it should be.

So what's the secret? The answer is all down to a simple choice. We can all choose to do certain things every day of our lives. Some things we do will make us unhappy and some things we choose to do will make us happier. By observing people, I have reasoned that if we follow a few basic 'Rules of life' we tend to get more done, shrug off adversity more easily, get more out of life and spread a little happiness around us as we go. People who play by the Rules seem to bring their luck with them, light up a room when they enter, have more enthusiasm for life and cope better.

So what follows are my Rules of life. They aren't set in stone, aren't secret or difficult. And they are based entirely on my observations of happy and successful people. I have noticed that those who are happy are those who follow most of them. Those who seem miserable are the ones who don't follow them. And the successful ones often don't even realize this is what they are doing – they are natural Rules Players. Whereas the less instinctive ones often feel something is missing and spend their entire life looking for something – often themselves – that will miraculously give their life meaning or fill some empty void within them. But the answer lies much closer to home – simple changes in behaviour are all that is required.

Can it really be that easy? No, of course not. To live by the Rules is never easy. If it was, we would all have stumbled on this a long time ago. It has to be hard to make it worthwhile. But, and this is the beauty of the Rules, they are all individually simple and attainable. You can aim high and go for them all or take one or two and start there. Me? No, I never get it all right, ever. I fall by the wayside as often as anyone else, but I do know what to do to get back up again. I know what I have to do to make my life make sense again.

By watching people I came to realize that all these Rules of life are sensible. Personally I love the sort of advice that begins 'Go quietly . . .' but I'm not sure how I'm supposed to do that. However, a bit of advice such as 'Clean your shoes before you go out' makes more sense to me because that is something I can do and, more importantly, is something in which I can immediately see the logic. Incidentally, I still feel polished shoes make a better impression than scruffy ones.

You won't actually find shoe polishing here, nor will you find anything inspirational and New Age, which doesn't mean those things don't count. It's just that I feel it is better to have realistic things we can do rather than uplifting clichés that may well be true – 'Time is a great healer', for example, and 'Love does conquer all' – but when you want things to do, they don't hit the button as far as I'm concerned.

What you will find is good old-fashioned common sense. There is nothing here you don't already know. This book isn't a revelation, it's a reminder. It reminds you that the Rules of life are universal, obvious, simple. Do them, they work.

But what about those who don't do them and still seem successful? Well, I'm sure we all know people who have acquired great wealth and who are ruthless, unpleasant, dictatorial and sail morally pretty close to the wind. And if that is what you want, it is attainable. But I'm assuming you want to be able to sleep nights, live with yourself and be a thoroughly nice person. And the beauty of all this is that it is entirely down to personal choice. We all choose every day whether we are on the side of the angels or the beasts. The Rules of life help you choose to be on the side of the angels, but it's not compulsory. Personally, when I go to sleep at night, I like to do a quick recap of my day and then, hopefully, I can say to myself 'Yep, good day, did OK', and feel proud of what I've achieved, rather than feeling regretful and dissatisfied with my actions and life. I like to go to sleep feeling I've made a difference, been kind to people rather than hurting them, spread a little happiness, had some fun and generally got nearer to 10 than 1 out of 10 for good behaviour.

The Rules of life aren't about making lots of money and being incredibly successful (you might need to read *The Rules of Work* for that). It is quite simply about how you feel inside, how you affect people around you, what sort of a friend, partner and parent you are, what sort of impact you make on the world, and what sort of impression you leave in your wake.

I regard my books, sometimes, a little like children. I pat them on the head, wipe their nose and send them out into the world. I like to know how they've got on. So if *The Rules of Life* makes a difference to you, or you have a Rule or two of your own that I've missed, I'm always interested in hearing from you. You can post your very own Rules on my Facebook page at www.facebook.com/richardtemplar

Richard Templar

Acknowledgements

I would like to thank all the readers who have emailed me over the years with comments on my books, and especially those who have contributed ideas to this new edition of *The Rules of Life*. In particular, may I thank:

Nicola Betts
Neil Duggan
Zakia Moulaoui
Daniel Nortey
Jalaj Soni
Elif Vatanoğlu
and Donna the pizza lady

RULES
FOR YOU

I've divided the main part of *The Rules of Life* into four areas – you, your partner, your family and friends, and your social circle and the wider world (including work) – to represent the four unconscious circles we all draw around ourselves.

Let's begin with the most important of these, the Rules for ourselves – personal Rules, Rules for us. These are the Rules that will help get us out of bed in the mornings, face the world with a positive air and navigate our way safely and successfully through our day, no matter what may arise. These are the Rules that will help reduce stress levels, give us the right kind of outlook, encourage us to set our own standards and have goals to aim for.

I guess that for each and every one of us, these Rules will have to be adapted to take into account our upbringing, our age and our situation. We all need to have personal standards to live up to. They will vary from person to person, but it is vitally important to have them. Without them we are adrift and unable to monitor how we are doing. With them we have a firm centre, somewhere we can get back to, somewhere to touch base and recharge. They are our benchmark for personal progress.

But it's not all about standards; it's also about lightening up, having fun, enjoying life.

Keep it under your hat

You are about to become a Rules Player. You are about to embark on a life-changing adventure, possibly, if you choose to accept your mission. You are about to discover ways to become positive, happier, more successful in everything you do. So there's no need to say anything to anybody about it. Keep quiet. No one likes a smart arse. That's it. First Rule: keep it under your hat.

There may well be times when you do want to talk to other people about what you're doing because, quite naturally, you want to share it with somebody. Well, you can't and you don't. Let them find out for themselves with no clues from you. You may think this unfair but it is actually fairer than you believe. If you tell them, they'll shy away. And quite rightly so – we all hate being preached at. It's a bit like when you give up smoking and suddenly find this new healthier way of living and you simply have to convert all your old smoking friends. Trouble is, they aren't ready to quit yet and you find they label you as smug or a prig or, even worse, an ex-smoker. And how we all hate those.

So the first Rule is, quite simply, don't preach, propagate, try to convert, shout from the rooftops or even mention this.

You will get a warm glow from changing your attitude to life and having people ask what it is you have done, are doing, and you can say that it's nothing, merely a sunny day and you feel better/happier/livelier/jollier/whatever. There is no need to go into any detail because that's not really what people want to know. In fact it's exactly the opposite of what they want to know. It's a bit like when someone asks how you are. What they really want to hear is just the one word, 'Fine'. Even if you are in the very pits of despair, that's all they want to hear because anything more requires commitment on their part. And for a casual 'How are you?' that's most certainly not what they want. What they want is just 'Fine'. And then they can be about their business without any further involvement. If you don't say 'Fine', but instead unburden yourself, they will back off pretty quickly.

And it's the same with being a Rules Player. No one really wants to know, so keep quiet. How do I know? Because when I wrote *The Rules of Work*, which turned a lot of people on to the ability to be successful in the workplace without having to resort to underhand means, I suggested the same thing and found it worked. Just get on with it, do it quietly and go about your daily life happily and smugly without having to tell anyone anything.

> # DON'T PREACH, PROPAGATE
> # OR TRY TO CONVERT

You'll get older but not necessarily wiser

There is an assumption that as we get older we will get wiser; not true I'm afraid. The rule is we carry on being just as daft, still making plenty of mistakes. It's just that we make new ones, different ones. We do learn from experience and may not make the same mistakes again, but there is a whole new pickle jar of fresh ones just lying in wait for us to trip up and fall into. The secret is to accept this and not to beat yourself up when you do make new ones. The Rule really is: be kind to yourself when you do muck things up. Be forgiving and accept that it's all part of that growing older but no wiser routine.

Looking back, we can always see the mistakes we made, but we fail to see the ones looming up. Wisdom isn't about not making mistakes, but about learning to escape afterwards with our dignity and sanity intact.

When we are young, ageing seems to be something that happens to, well, old people. But it does happen to us all and we have no choice but to embrace it and roll with it. Whatever we do and whoever we are, the fact is we are going to get older. And this ageing process does seem to speed up as we get older.

You can look at it this way – the older you get, the more areas you've covered to make mistakes in. There will always be new areas of experience where we have no guidelines and where we'll handle things badly, overreact, get it wrong. And the more flexible we are, the more adventurous, the more life-embracing, then the more new avenues there will be to explore – and make mistakes in of course.

As long as we look back and see where we went wrong and resolve not to repeat such mistakes, there is little else we need to do. Remember that any Rules that apply to you also apply to everyone else around you. They are all getting older too. And not any wiser particularly. Once you accept this, you'll be more forgiving and kinder towards yourself and others.

Finally, yes, time does heal and things do get better as you get older. After all, the more mistakes you've made, the less likely that you'll come up with new ones. The best thing is that if you get a lot of your mistakes over and done with early on in life, there will be less to learn the hard way later on. And that's what youth is all about, a chance to make all the mistakes you can and get them out of the way.

WISDOM ISN'T ABOUT NOT MAKING MISTAKES BUT ABOUT LEARNING TO ESCAPE AFTERWARDS WITH OUR DIGNITY AND SANITY INTACT

RULE 3

Accept what is done is done

People make mistakes. Sometimes very serious ones. As often as not, the mistakes aren't deliberate or personal. Sometimes people just don't know what they are doing. This means that if, in the past, people have behaved badly towards you, it wasn't necessarily because they meant to be horrid, but because they were as naïve, as foolish, as human as the rest of us. They made mistakes in the way they brought you up or finished a relationship with you or whatever, not because they wanted to do it that way, but because they didn't know any different.

If you want to, you can let go of any feelings of resentment, of regret, of anger. You can accept that you are a fabulous human being *because* of all the bad things that have happened to you, not in spite of them. What is done is done and you need to just get on with things. Don't use the labels 'good' and 'bad'. Yes, I know some of it is indeed bad, but it is how we let it affect us that is the real 'bad'. You could let all these things get you down, fizzle away internally like some emotional acid making you ill and resentful and stuck. Try instead to let them go, embrace them as character forming and in general as positive rather than negative.

On paper I had a seriously dysfunctional childhood and for a while was resentful. I blamed my bizarre upbringing for all that was weak or dispirited or badly formed in me. It's so easy to do. But once I accepted that what was done was done, and that I could choose to forgive and get on with my life, things improved enormously. For at least one of my siblings this was not the route they chose, and they carried on building up the resentment until it overwhelmed them.

WHAT IS DONE IS DONE AND YOU NEED TO JUST GET ON WITH THINGS

For me it was essential, if I wanted more out of my life, to embrace all the bad things as being an important part of me and to move on. In fact I wanted them to fuel me into my future, to become positive to such an extent that I couldn't imagine being me without them. Now, if given the choice, I wouldn't change a thing. Yes, looking back, it was tough being the kid I was, living the life I did, but it has certainly helped make me me.

I think the change occurred once I realized that even if I could get in front of me all the people who had 'done me wrong', there would still be nothing they could do. I could shout at them, berate them, rant at them, but there would be nothing they could do to make amends or put things right. They too would have to accept that what's done is done. There is no going back, only forwards. Make it a motto for life – keep moving forwards.

RULE 4

Accept yourself

If you accept that what's done is done, you are left with yourself exactly as you are. You can't go back and change anything, so you've got to work with what you've got. I'm not suggesting anything New Age here such as love yourself – that's far too ambitious. No, let's begin with simple accepting. Accepting is easy because it is exactly what it says – accepting. You don't have to improve or change or strive for perfection. Quite the opposite. Just accept.

That means accepting all the warts and emotional lumps and bumps, the bad bits, the weaknesses and the rest of it. This doesn't mean we are happy with everything about ourselves, or that we are going to be lazy and lead a bad life. We are going to accept the way we are, initially, and then build on that. What we are *not* going to do is beat ourselves up because we don't like some bits. Yes, we can change lots but that will come later. We're only up to Rule 4 here.

> YOU DON'T HAVE TO
> IMPROVE OR CHANGE OR
> STRIVE FOR PERFECTION.
> QUITE THE OPPOSITE.
> JUST ACCEPT

This has to be a Rule because there can be no choice here. We have to accept that we are the way we are – the result of everything that has happened. It all just is. You, like me, like all of us, are human. That means you're pretty complex. You come fully loaded with desires, anguish, sins, pettiness at times, mistakes, ill temper, rudeness, deviation, hesitation and repetition. That's what makes a human being so wonderful, the complexity.

None of us can ever be perfect. We start with what we've got and who we are, and then we can only make a choice, each day, to strive for some kind of better. And that's all we can ask of ourselves – to make that choice. To be awake and aware, to be ready to do the right thing. And accept that some days you aren't going to make it. Some days you will, like all of us, fall far short. That's OK, don't beat yourself up. Pick yourself up and start again. Accept that you will fail from time to time and that you are human.

I know it can be hard at times, but once you have picked up the gauntlet of becoming a Rules Player, you're well on the path to improvement. Stop picking faults with yourself, or giving yourself a hard time. Instead, accept that you are what you are. You're doing the best you can at this point in time, so give yourself a pat on the back and press on.

Know what counts and what doesn't

Being here counts. Being kind and considerate counts. Getting through each day without seriously offending anyone or hurting anyone counts. Having the latest technology doesn't.

Sorry, I don't have a downer on technology. In fact, I probably have pretty much all the latest gizmos. I just (a) don't overly rely too much on any of them and (b) see them all as useful tools rather than having any intrinsic meaning in themselves, in a status symbol or one-up-personship kind of way.

Doing something useful with your life counts. Going shopping because you're bored doesn't. Yes, by all means go shopping, but see what you do as counting or not counting, being real or not being real, having real value or not, being of some benefit or not. This does not mean chucking it all up and going off to some fly-infested swamp to work with the locals and catch malaria – although that in itself *would* count, but you don't have to go to quite those extremes to make your life meaningful.

I guess this Rule means focusing on what is important to you in your life, and making positive changes to ensure you feel happy with what you are dedicating your life to (see Rule 6). This doesn't mean long-term plans mapped out to the smallest detail. It means knowing, roughly, where you are going and what you are doing. Awake rather than asleep. A fellow author, Tim Freke, calls it 'lucid living'* – a perfect term for what we are talking about.

---

* *Lucid Living* by Tim Freke (Books for Burning, 2005).

There are some things in this life that are important and a whole lot of things that aren't. It doesn't take too much trouble to work out which are which. And there are a whole lot more things that don't count, aren't really important, to choose from. I'm not saying we can't have trivia in our lives – we can and it's fine. Just don't go mistaking the trivia for what is really important. Having time for loved ones and friends is important, watching the latest soap isn't. Repaying a debt is important, what brand of washing powder you use isn't. Nurturing your children and teaching them real values is important, dressing them in designer fashion isn't. You get the idea. Think about what you do that counts – and do more of it.

> ## THERE ARE SOME THINGS IN THIS LIFE THAT ARE IMPORTANT AND A WHOLE LOT OF THINGS THAT AREN'T

RULE 6

Dedicate your life to something

To know what counts and what doesn't, you have to know what you are dedicating your life to. There are, of course, no right or wrong answers to this one as it's a very personal choice – but it's really useful to have an answer, rather than not really knowing.

As an example, my own life has been driven by two things: (a) someone once told me that if my soul or spirit was the only thing I was likely to be taking with me when I went, then it ought to be the best thing I had; (b) my curious upbringing.

The first one isn't, for me at least, in any way religious. It just struck a chord with me, triggered something. Whatever it was I was taking with me, then perhaps I ought to do a bit of work on it. Make sure it really is the very best thing about me. That got me thinking. How on earth do you go about that? The answer still is that I haven't got a clue. I have explored and experimented, learned and made mistakes, been a seeker and a follower, read and observed and wrestled with this great problem all my life. How do you go about improving your life on that level? I think the only conclusion I have come to is to live as decent a life as possible, to go through causing as little damage as possible, to treat everyone with whom I come into contact with respect and dignity. It's something to dedicate my life to and it works for me.

And how can my curious upbringing cause me to focus on what I am dedicating my life to? Well, having had a 'dysfunctional' upbringing and having chosen to let it motivate me rather than affect me, I am acutely aware that many people also need to throw off that feeling of being badly affected by what has gone before. This is what I dedicate my life to. Yes, it might be crazy; I might be crazy. But at least I have something I can focus on, something (for me) that counts.

Now none of this is big stuff and by that I mean I don't go around with this emblazoned on my forehead – 'Templar dedicates his life to . . .' sort of thing. It's more that, quietly, in my heart, I have something that I can devote my attention to. It's a yardstick by which I can measure (a) how I'm doing, (b) what I'm doing and (c) where I'm going. You don't need to trumpet it. You don't need to tell anyone (see Rule 1). You don't even need to think it out in too much detail. A simple internal mission statement will do. Disney's mission for example is: 'To make people happy'. Decide what it is you are dedicating your life to. It makes the rest much easier.

> ## A SIMPLE INTERNAL MISSION STATEMENT WILL DO

Be flexible in your thinking

Once your thinking gets crystallized, rigid, formed, you've lost the battle. Once you think you have all the answers, you might as well hang up your boots. Once you get set in your ways, you're already part of history.

To get the most out of life you have to keep all your options open, keep your thinking and life flexible. You have to be ready to roll as the storm breaks – and by golly it always breaks when you least expect it. The instant you are established in a set pattern, you set yourself up for being knocked off-course. You might need to examine your thinking pretty closely to understand what I mean. Flexible thinking is a bit like mental martial arts – being ready to duck and weave, dodge and flow. Try to see life not as the enemy, but as a friendly sparring partner. If you are flexible you'll have fun. If you stand your ground you're likely to get knocked about a bit.

We all have set patterns in life. We like to label ourselves as this or that and are quite proud of our opinions and beliefs. We all like to read a set paper, watch the same sorts of TV programmes or movies, go to the same sort of shops every time, eat the sort of food that suits us, wear the same type of clothes. And all this is fine. But if we cut ourselves off from all other possibilities, we become boring, rigid, hardened – and thus likely to get knocked about a bit.

You have to see life as a series of adventures. Each adventure is a chance to have fun, learn something, explore the world, expand your circle of friends and experience, and broaden your horizons. Shutting down to adventure means exactly that – you are shut down.

The second you are offered an opportunity to have an adventure, to change your thinking, to step outside of yourself, go for it and see what happens. If this thought scares you, remember that you can always go back into your shell the second it's over, if you want to.

But even saying yes to every opportunity isn't set in stone as a rule, because that would be inflexible. The really flexible thinkers know when to say no as well as when to say yes.

If you want to know how flexible your thinking is, here are a couple of tests. Are the books by the side of your bed the same sorts of books you've always read? Have you found yourself saying anything like 'I don't know any people like that' or 'I don't go to those kind of places'? If so, then perhaps it's time to broaden your mind and take the shackles off your thinking.

> TRY TO SEE LIFE NOT AS THE
> ENEMY, BUT AS A FRIENDLY
> SPARRING PARTNER

RULE 8

Take an interest in the outside world

You may be wondering why this Rule is here and not in the section about the wider world. Well, this one is about *you*. Taking an interest in the outside world is about developing you for yourself, rather than for the world's benefit. I'm not suggesting you have to watch the news constantly, but by reading, listening and talking, we keep abreast of what is happening. Successful Rules Players don't get bogged down by the minutiae of their own lives; they don't live in a tiny bubble. Make it your mission to know what's going on in the world – in current events, music, fashion, science, movies, food, transport, even TV. Successful Rules Players are able to hold a conversation on pretty well everything and anything because they are interested in what's going on. You don't necessarily have to *own* the latest everything, but you should have a rough idea of what is changing, what's new and what's happening, both in your community and on the other side of the world.

And the benefits? Well, for starters it makes you more interesting as a person and it also keeps you young. I met an elderly woman in the post office the other day who was going on about PIN numbers, 'PIN numbers, PIN numbers, what do I want with PIN numbers at my age?' The short answer is that of course she needs them, she can't get her pension money without them. But it's more than that. It is terribly easy to sink into the, 'I've never done this before, I don't need to do it now' mentality. If we do this, we stand a good chance of really missing out.

The happiest, most well-balanced, most successful people in life are those who are part of something. Part of the world, not cut off from it. And the most interesting, stimulating people to be around are those who take a great interest in what's happening around them. Listening to the radio the other morning, the head of the American prison service was being interviewed and was talking about penal reform, a subject I have no interest in personally (I don't know anyone inside, over there). You could argue that I didn't need to know about the American prison service any more than the old woman needed to know about PIN numbers, but I felt more stimulated and alive and interested for it. And that can't be bad.

> **TAKING AN INTEREST IN THE OUTSIDE WORLD IS ABOUT DEVELOPING YOU, RATHER THAN FOR THE WORLD'S BENEFIT**

RULE 9

Be on the side of the angels, not the beasts

Every single day of our lives we are faced with an immense number of choices. And each and every one of them usually boils down to a simple choice between being on the side of the angels or the beasts. Which are you going to pick? Or did you not even realize what was going on? Let me explain. Every action we make has an effect on our family, people around us, society, the world in general. And that effect can be positive or detrimental – it's usually our choice. And sometimes it is a difficult choice. We get torn between what *we* want and what is good for others; personal satisfaction or magnanimity.

Look, no one said this was going to be easy. And making the decision to be on the side of the angels is often a tough call. But if we want to succeed in this life – and I measure success by how close we get to generating that self-satisfaction/happiness/contentment – then we consciously have to do this. This can be what we dedicate our lives to – angels and not beasts.

> **WE GET TORN BETWEEN WHAT *WE* WANT AND WHAT IS GOOD FOR OTHERS**

If you want to know if you have already made the choice, just do a quick check of how you feel and how you react if someone cuts in front of you in a line of traffic in the rush hour. Or when you're in a big hurry and someone stops to ask you for directions. Or if you have teenage children and one of them gets into trouble with the police. Or when you lend a friend money and they fail to pay it back. Or if your boss calls you a fool in front of the rest of your colleagues. Or your neighbour's trees start to encroach on your property. Or you hit your thumb with a hammer. Or, or, or. As I said, it is a choice we have to make every day, lots of times. And it has to become a conscious choice to be effective.

Now, the problem is that no one is going to tell you exactly what constitutes an angel or a beast. Here you are going to have to set your own parameters. But come on, it can't be that difficult. I think an awful lot of it is self-evident. Does it hurt or hinder? Are you part of the problem or the solution? Will things get better or worse if you do certain things? You have to make this choice for yourself alone.

It is your interpretation of what is an angel or beast that counts. There is no point in telling anyone else that they are on the side of the beasts, as they may have a totally different definition. What other people do is their choice and they won't thank you for telling them otherwise. You can of course watch, as an impassive, objective, observer, and think to yourself: 'I wouldn't have done it like that'. Or 'I think they just chose to be an angel'. Or even, 'Gosh, how beastly'. But you don't have to say anything.

Only dead fish swim with the stream

Life is difficult. And the Rule is to thank God* it is so. If it was all fluffy and easy we wouldn't be tested, tried, forged in the fire of life. We wouldn't grow or learn or change, or have a chance to rise above ourselves. If life were a series of lovely days, we'd soon get bored. If there was no rain, then there wouldn't be any feeling of great joy when it finally stopped and we could go to the beach. If it was all easy we couldn't get stronger.

So, be thankful it is a struggle some of the time, and recognize that only dead fish swim with the stream. For the rest of us there will be times when it's an uphill, upstream struggle. We will have to battle waterfalls, weirs and raging torrents. But we have no choice. We have to keep swimming or get swept away. And each flick of our tail, each surge of our fins makes us stronger and fitter, leaner and happier.

There is a statistic that suggests that for a lot of men, retirement is a really bad idea. Lots of them die within a relatively short time of handing in their briefcase.** They have ceased to swim against the current and get swept away. Keep swimming, little fish, keep swimming.

Try to see each setback as a chance to improve. They make you stronger, not weaker. You only get burdened with as much as you can carry – although I do appreciate that at times it may seem as if it's a whole lot more. And of course the struggles don't come to an end, but there are lulls in-between times – backwaters where we can rest for a while and enjoy the moment before the next obstacle gets thrown our way. And that's what

---

* Or whoever or whatever you choose to so thank. Don't write in.
** I don't know if this affects women just as adversely. You may write in.

life is, what it is meant to be: a series of struggles and lulls. And whatever situation you're in now, it's going to change. So what are you in? Lull or struggle? Rain or going to the beach? Learning or enjoying? Dead fish or healthy salmon?

AND THAT'S WHAT LIFE IS, WHAT IT IS MEANT TO BE: A SERIES OF STRUGGLES AND LULLS

RULE 11

Be the last to raise your voice

For me this is a really hard one. I do love to have a good shout. I came from a big robust family where shouting was a way of life and the only way to get yourself heard, get any attention or to make a point. Dysfunctional? Yes. Noisy? Yes. Helpful? Probably not.

One of my sons has inherited the shouting gene and he is very good at it. The temptation is to join in. Luckily this Rule is be the last to raise your voice, so I do have a get-out clause. If he shouts first, I'm allowed to shout back. But I do try really hard not to. For me, shouting in any form is a bad thing, a sign that I have lost control, lost the argument. The son of a vicar once saw his father's sermon notes and in the margin he had pencilled, 'Shout here, argument weak'. I think this just about sums it all up.

But I have shouted at various times and invariably I regret each and every occasion. I know I've dined out on the time I was very shouty in a well-known high street electrical chain over a damaged DVD player. At that time I did get my own way, but the reality is that it was a bad thing and deep down I'm quite ashamed of myself.

SHOUTING IS A SIGN THAT
I HAVE LOST CONTROL

So what do you do if you too have inherited the shouty gene like me? I find that I have to walk away to stop the inevitable decline into shouting in a challenging situation. Tough one, especially if you know you're right. There are so many things that make us shout, so many situations where we feel that a judicious loss of temper will get us our own way. But we are dealing with real live human beings who have their own feelings, and shouting is not justified – even if they start it first.

There are two situations where people lose their temper – justified and manipulative. The first is where you run over their foot with your car and refuse to apologize or acknowledge you have done anything wrong. In this situation they are allowed to shout. The second situation is where people use anger to get their own way – a sort of emotional blackmail. You are allowed to ignore them, or to be assertive to control the situation. You are not allowed to shout back.

I know, I know, there are all sorts of situations where shouting seems appropriate – the dog is stealing the Sunday dinner; the kids won't tidy their room; your computer has crashed again and the repair department won't fix it quickly enough; the local hooligans are adorning your wall, again; after going through the umpteen options over and over again you fail to get through to the switchboard after holding for 20 minutes; they put up the closed sign just as you get to the counter; someone is clearly being stupid and deliberately choosing to misunderstand you.

And on and on and on. But if you take this Rule as a simple 'I don't do shouting', it becomes an easy benchmark to stick to. You get known as someone who is incredibly calm no matter what is happening. Calm people get trusted. Calm people get relied on. Calm people get looked up to and given responsibility. Calm people last longer.

RULE 12

Be your own adviser

Deep down within all of us is a fount of wisdom. This is called intuition. Listening to your intuition is a slow learnt process. It starts by recognizing that tiny inner voice or feeling that will tell you when you've done something you shouldn't have. It's an incredibly still, quiet voice and needs silence and concentration to hear it properly to begin with.

You might like to call it your conscience if you like, but deep down you know when you've done something bad. You know when you've got to apologize, make amends, put things right. You know. And I know you know. I know because we all know. There's no getting away from it.

Once you start listening to that inner voice, or feeling the feeling, you'll find it can help. It will become more than a mindless parrot perched on your shoulder, chanting 'You messed up again' after the event. The key is when you hear your intuition telling you whether something is the right thing to do or not – *before* you do it.

> YOU KNOW. AND I KNOW
> YOU KNOW. I KNOW
> BECAUSE WE ALL KNOW

Try running stuff past your inner you before doing things and see what reaction you get. Once you get used to this, you'll find it easier. Imagine, in any situation, that you have a small child standing at your side and you have to explain things to them. Imagine they ask questions – 'Why are you doing that? What's right and wrong? Should we do this?' – and you have to answer. Only in this situation you ask the questions and you answer yourself. And you'll find you already know everything there is to know and everything you'll ever need to know.

Listen, and it's all there. If you are going to trust any adviser, who will it be? It makes sense for it to be *you* because you have all the facts, all the experience, all the knowledge at your fingertips. No one else has. No one can get inside you and see exactly what's going on.

Quick point of clarification here. When I say listen, I don't mean listen to what goes on in your head. Now that really is where madness lies. No, I mean a stiller, quieter voice. For some it's more a feeling than a voice – what we sometimes call gut instinct. And even if it is a voice, a lot of the time it doesn't speak at all – unlike our mind which babbles on incessantly – and if it does, you can miss it in the torrent of words that our mind produces.

This isn't about predicting what's going to happen. You won't discover which horse will win the 3.30 at Chepstow or who'll score in the Cup Final. No, this is the important stuff. What we're about to do, big decisions we have to make, why we are behaving in the way we are. You already know the answer, if you ask yourself.

No fear, no surprise, no hesitation, no doubt

Where does this come from? It's from a seventeenth-century samurai warrior. This was his four-point key to successful living – and swordsmanship.

- **No fear**. There should be nothing in this life that you are afraid of. If there is, you might need to do some work on overcoming that fear. Here I have to confess to a certain fear of heights. I avoid high places if I can. Recently, owing to leaky gutters, I had to crawl out on our roof – three floors up with a very long drop on one side. I gritted my teeth and kept repeating, 'No fear, no fear, no fear', until the job was done. Oh yes, and of course I didn't look down. Whatever your fear, face it head on and defeat it.

- **No surprise**. Life seems to be full of them, doesn't it? You're going along swimmingly and suddenly something huge rears up ahead of you. But if you look carefully, there were clues all along the way that it was going to happen. No surprise there then. Whatever your situation now, it is going to change. No surprises there. So why does life seem to surprise us then? Because we are asleep half the time. Wake up and nothing can sneak up on you.

- **No hesitation**. Weigh up the odds and then just get on with it. If you hang back, the opportunity will have passed. If you spend too long thinking, you'll never make a move. Once we have looked at the options, we make a choice, a decision and then go for it. That's the secret. No hesitation means not waiting around for other people to help out or make up our minds for us. No hesitation means if there is a certain inevitability about a situation then just throw yourself in head first and enjoy the ride. If there is nothing to be done then waiting doesn't help.

- **No doubt**. Once you have made up your mind about something, don't go over it again and again. Stop thinking and enjoy – relax and let go. Stop worrying. Tomorrow will come along as certainly as it can. There is no doubt about life. It just is. Be confident. Be committed. Be sure of yourself. Once you have committed yourself to a set course, a path, a plan, then follow it through. Have no doubt it was the right thing to do and no doubt that you will succeed. Get on with it and trust your judgement completely.

> # WAKE UP AND NOTHING
> # CAN SNEAK UP ON YOU

RULE 14

I wish I'd done that – and I will

Regrets, I've had a few . . . You might be expecting me to say there's no room for regrets or 'if onlys'. As it happens, they can be very useful – if you choose to use them to make a difference going forward.

There are three types of 'I wish I'd done that' scenarios. The first is when you genuinely feel you didn't capitalize on an opportunity, or that you missed out on something. The second is when you see somebody who's done something great and you wish it had been you. The final type is not you, but the others – the people who hang around with a sort of permanent 'I could have been a contender' mentality. If only I'd had the chances, the lucky breaks, the opportunities. For this last group, the bad news is that even if Lady Luck had come up and bitten them on the bum they'd still have missed it.

When it comes to looking at what others have achieved, this world is divided into those who look at others enviously and those who look at others as a motivational tool. If you find yourself saying, 'I wish I had done that/thought that/been there/ seen that/experienced that/met them/understood that', then you need to learn to follow it up with a 'And now, I will . . .'

In many cases the thing you wished you'd done might not be out of the question – even if it's not exactly as you would have done it previously. For example, if you're thinking 'I wish I'd taken a year out before university and travelled to China like so and so did', then you're clearly not going to be able to reverse time. But could you get a sabbatical for six months and go now? Could you take a longer-than-usual holiday and go (with family if necessary)? Or how about making firm plans that when you retire you'll put this at the top of your 'to do' list?

> # THE WORLD IS DIVIDED INTO THOSE WHO LOOK AT OTHERS ENVIOUSLY AND THOSE WHO LOOK AT OTHERS AS A MOTIVATIONAL TOOL

Obviously, if the regret is that you didn't win an Olympic 400m gold medal, because you gave up athletics at 14, it's not going to happen if you're now 34. What you can do is resolve not to let any more opportunities pass you by. So you can choose to book those scuba diving lessons and, in doing so, ensure that you won't be saying 'I wish I'd learned to dive' in another 20 years' time.

It's OK to give up

You know how you sometimes hear stories about people who have failed their driving test 35 times? Much as you admire their persistence, don't you sometimes wonder why they don't just give up? These are clearly people who just aren't cut out to drive big, heavy, dangerous lumps of machinery around streets full of children, old people, dogs and lamp posts. Even if they do finally pass, there's a feeling that it's probably a fluke, and you probably still wouldn't want to be a passenger on their next trip.

Actually, if these people held their hands up (as some do) and said, 'You know what? This isn't me. I'm going to get a bicycle and a bus season ticket', I would applaud their ability to see what was staring them in the face. I wouldn't call them quitters, or criticize their lack of determination or drive.* They'd simply be getting the message loud and clear, and having the good sense not to ignore it.

Sometimes we head off down the wrong path in life, often with the best motives. Maybe there's no knowing it's the wrong path until we try it. There's no shame in admitting it once we realize it's not getting us where we want to be. When you realize this college course isn't right for you, or that you don't have what it takes to do this job well, or that your move to a new city isn't working out, or that the hours you put into being on the local council put too much strain on your family, it takes guts to say so. That's not quitting. That's courage.

Quitting is when you give up because you don't want to put in the effort, you can't be bothered, you don't like hard work, you're scared of failure. We Rules Players don't quit. We harden our resolve and we get on with the job without complaint.

---

* Sorry, couldn't resist that one.

However, a good Rules Player knows when they're beat. If the world is telling you that you took a wrong turning, you can admit it honestly and put yourself on a different track. No one can be brilliant at everything, and sometimes you have to try things to find out whether you can do them. And maybe you can't.

A few years ago a leading UK government minister resigned from her post, famously saying that she was simply 'not up to the job'. Now, I'd never really rated her up to that point, but she rose hugely in my estimation – and that of many others – for that admission. That took guts. Maybe she wasn't great at leading a government department, but she was certainly in a different league from most politicians when it comes to honesty, courage and self-knowledge. She's an outstanding example of the fact that if you give up in the right way at the right time, you're showing strength of character, not weakness.

> # A GOOD RULES PLAYER KNOWS WHEN THEY'RE BEAT

Count to ten – or recite 'Baa baa black sheep'

Every now and then someone or something is really going to get your goat. But you're a Rules Player now and you're not going to lose your temper any more. How, exactly? The answer is in fact one of those old pearls of wisdom. You get in the habit of counting to ten under your breath while you hope and pray that the feeling of impending rage will subside. It invariably does for me, and gives me those vital seconds to regain my composure and remember where I am and who I am. Once I have collected my wits and calmed down, I can find an appropriate response.

But that counting to ten is essential. 'Old hat', I hear you say. Yep, but it works. You don't like it? Then you are most welcome to find something else to recite under your breath. A poem perhaps, but it has to be a short one. That's why I suggested 'Baa baa black sheep'.

> ONCE I HAVE COLLECTED MY WITS AND CALMED DOWN, I CAN FIND AN APPROPRIATE RESPONSE

Or you could try 'I must go down to the sea again, to the lonely sea and the sky, I left my pants and socks there and I wonder if they're dry'.* That might make you laugh as well as calming you down.

Someone asks you a question and you're not sure of the answer? Take ten before you answer. They'll all think you incredibly wise and considered and thoughtful. (Don't tell them if you are actually reciting 'Baa baa black sheep'.) It's a variant on 'Engage brain before opening mouth' too – that extended pause can save endless trouble.

If you find yourself in a confrontational situation, taking a quiet ten can help enormously. I was once in a rough part of a town but very hungry so I ventured into a fish and chip shop. As I was being served, the 'rough diamond' behind me whispered that I should be very careful when I left the shop. I asked why and he said that I would be relieved of my food when I got outside by the local lads who were all sitting on a brick wall. 'Saves waiting in the queue', he confided.

I left the shop with trepidation – no, wait, it was actually fear. But I buttoned up my coat, took a deep breath and stood there looking at the youths. I counted to ten slowly while we all eyed each other up and then I walked towards them very purposefully. As I got to them, still counting, they turned away and I was left alone. God, those fish and chips tasted wonderful!

---

* Big apology to John Masefield for that but due credit to Spike Milligan.

Change what you can change, let go of the rest

Time is short. This is another of those facts you can't escape; it's a given. If time is short then it makes sense not to go wasting any of it, not a single lovely drop of it. It's my observation that the successful people in this life are the ones who wring every last ounce of satisfaction and energy out of life. They do that by practising this simple Rule. They pay attention to what, in their life, they have some control over and they simply, economically (time-wise), let go of the rest.

If someone asks you directly for help, then that's something you can do – or not, as you choose. If the whole world asks you for help, then there is very little you can do. Beating yourself up over it is counter-productive and such a waste of time. Now I'm not saying to stop caring about things or to walk away from those in need. In fact quite the opposite in many ways, but there are areas in which you can make a personal difference and other areas where you'll never even make a dent.

If you waste time struggling to change stuff that is obviously never going to be changed, then life will whizz past and you'll miss it. If, on the other hand, you dedicate yourself personally to things you can change, areas where you can make a difference, then life becomes richer and more fulfilled. And the more rich it is, curiously, the more time you seem to have.

Obviously if lots of us get together we can change pretty well anything, but this is a Rule for you – these are your personal set – and thus this is about what *you* can change.

DEDICATE YOURSELF PERSONALLY TO THINGS YOU CAN CHANGE, AREAS WHERE YOU CAN MAKE A DIFFERENCE

If you have the ear of a president or prime minister, you might be able to shape policy that affects the entire nation. If you have the ear of the Pope, you might have a hand in shaping the next papal bull. If you have the ear of a general, you might avert a war. If you have the ear of an editor, you might get your name in print. If you have the ear of the head waiter, you might get the best table. And so on and so on. So whose ear have you got? What influence do you have and what change can you effect by using that influence?

Often the only ear we have is our own. The only definite influence we have is over ourselves. The only thing we can really, really change is exactly that – ourselves. Wonderful. What an opportunity to do some good. What a chance to make a real contribution. Begin with ourselves and let it spread outwards. This way we don't have to waste time preaching to those who won't listen. We don't have to waste effort or energy or resources on things over which we have no control and no certainty of any success. By changing ourselves though we can be assured of a result. Result.

Aim to be the very best at everything you do – not second best

Wow. What a tall order. This is a seriously difficult thing to aim for – and deliberately so. If you go to work, then do your job as well as is humanly possible. If you are a parent, be the very best parent possible. If you are a gardener, be the very best gardener you can be. Because if you aren't, then what are you aiming for? And why? If you set out to do something, anything, and you are deliberately aiming for second best, how sad is that? This Rule is really simple, really easy. Let's take parenting, for example. What is the very best way of parenting possible? There are of course no right or wrong answers here; it's entirely a subjective assessment. What do *you* think the very best parenting means? Good. Now, are you going to aim for less than that? Of course not.

And the same is true for everything you do. You aim to be the very best that *you* think is possible. Once you become the judge, the panel of experts, it is very easy to live up to those expectations because they are entirely yours. No one else can say whether you have failed or succeeded. No one else can set the criteria for what you are about to embark on.

Look, maybe this is a trick. If only you can judge whether you have succeeded, then obviously you are going to score 10 out of 10 every time. Aren't you? Probably not. It is amazing how tough we are on ourselves, when no one is looking. If we are only cheating ourselves, then we realize there simply isn't any point to it.

The most marvellous thing about setting your own standards is that no one else can judge; no one else can get their sticky little fingers on what, for you, is right or wrong, good or bad. How liberating is that? Infinitely. Having established that you'll aim for the very best and you've set the standards of what that is, all you have to do is periodically check back to that standard to see how you are doing.

None of this has to be incredibly detailed. For instance, your view of being the best parent could be as simple as 'I'll always be there for them'. You don't have to provide details, even if it is just for yourself, of how many times a day you'll tell them you love them, or whether you make sure they wear clean socks every day. No, your aim is simply 'To be there for them, always', and that is your very, very best. Now if you fail it is only because you weren't there for them. Failing is fine. Aiming for second best isn't.

All you have to do is consciously think about what you are doing and then aim for that, the best. The secret is to be aware of what you are doing and have some sort of benchmark where you, and only you, monitor your performance. Make your goals, your aims, simple and obviously attainable. Make sure you know what is, for you, best and second best.

> # FAILING IS FINE. AIMING
> # FOR SECOND BEST ISN'T

Don't expect to be perfect

OK, so you're aiming to be the very best at everything. But what if you fail? So long as you tried, that's alright. Who have you ever met who never failed at anything, however small? You're allowed to be human you know. In fact, you're actively encouraged to be human. Don't try to set yourself above everyone else – the rest of us fail from time to time.

If you're not a perfectionist in any way – sloppy, haphazard, unorganized, messy and with a 'so what' attitude – please skip this section. But I hardly know anyone like that. I have a friend who is a silversmith. His house is a tip, his personal life is all over the place, but every piece of jewellery he turns out has to be exactly right. Most of us have some perfectionist tendencies.

My jeweller friend is quite right that every piece of work has to be perfect (certainly at his prices). If any piece is faulty he shouldn't sell it. But that doesn't mean that he should beat himself up for having failed. He can just recognize that not everything works out, and get to work on the next piece.

I can't stand people who seem perfect. They make me feel inadequate. And that's not a nice way to go through life, is it? Going round making other people feel inadequate? So let's have none of it. Let's all aim to be the best, but acknowledge that it won't always happen. Just like gemstones, it's the flaws, the weaknesses, the imperfections that lend character. A flaw in a gemstone may detract from its value (though not always) but it also proves that it's genuine.

You are the sum total of everything that has happened in your life. The successes and the failures, the achievements and the mistakes. If you were to take any of the imperfect bits out of that equation, you wouldn't be you.

This Rule really does belong with the previous one, because I'm not saying that you can be uncommitted and half-hearted about everything you do because you don't need to be perfect. And as a Rules Player I'm sure you wouldn't take it that way. The point is that so long as you're aiming for the best, you shouldn't beat yourself up when you don't always make it. Not only that, but you should celebrate your flaws and imperfections as an important and necessary part of you. This is an attitude that will make you a lot more fun to be around, I can tell you.

> **CELEBRATE YOUR FLAWS AND IMPERFECTIONS AS AN IMPORTANT AND NECESSARY PART OF YOU**

RULE 20

Don't be afraid to dream

This may seem incredibly obvious, incredibly easy, but you would be surprised how many people seriously limit their dreams. They're *your* dreams for heaven's sake. There should be no limit to them. Plans have to be realistic; dreams don't.

I worked in the casino business for many years and was always intrigued that 'punters' (what we should really call 'customers') could never see it: that they would always lose because they wouldn't limit their losses but would always limit their winnings. Don't ask me why. I guess addicted gamblers are seriously not well. They'd go in with the right attitude – 'I'll just lose this fiver and then pack it in'. Result: they'd lose the fiver and cash a cheque to chase it. Then another to chase the lost cheque. And another.

> ## PLANS HAVE TO BE REALISTIC;
> ## DREAMS DON'T

I'm not advocating gambling by the way – not now, not ever; it's really not a good idea, believe me. The point is that people limit their dreams the way they limit their winnings. And yet dreams are at worst harmless. Don't limit them! You are allowed to dream as high, as wide, as big, as extravagant, as impossible, as wacky, as silly, as bizarre, as unrealistically nonsensical as you want.

You are allowed to wish for anything you want as well. Look, wishes and dreams are all private affairs. There are no wish police, no dream doctors who are on the rampage looking out for unrealistic demands. It is a private thing between you and . . . that's it. Between you and absolutely no one else at all.

The only note of caution here – and I do speak from personal experience – is be very careful of what you do wish for, what you dream of, because it might just come true. And where would you be then?

A lot of people think their dreams have to be realistic to be worth dreaming about. But that's a plan and that is something quite different. I have plans and I take logical steps to make them come to fruition. Dreams are allowed to be so improbable that they are never likely to come true. And don't go thinking you'll never achieve anything by sitting around day-dreaming all day. Some of the most successful people have also been those who have dared to dream the most. It isn't a coincidence.

RULE 21

If you're going to jump off a bridge, make sure you know how deep the water is

Me, I've always been a risk-taker. Too much of a risk-taker some might say. In the long term I haven't regretted the things I've done in life because they've made me who I am, and anyway you never know where the alternative would have got you. In the short term, however, I have often caught myself thinking, 'You numbskull! Why didn't you see that coming?'

The answer, of course, is because I didn't check how deep the water was before I jumped. There was the time I gave up a very good steady job to become a writer. Didn't think about how long it would take to make any money as a writer.* Didn't plan out whether my savings would last. Didn't calculate what the mortgage, bills, weekly shopping, car, pet food and all the rest would cost me with a new lifestyle. Well, eventually I started to make a living from my writing, but there were some pretty sticky years first I can tell you.

I've always been terrified of ending up like those people I know who never take risks and who never go anywhere, change, grow, do anything, realize their dreams. I've seen it too often and I don't want my name added to the list, thank you. But over the years I've noticed that the people who are really happy are the ones who take risks, sure, but they look ahead first. Not looking for excuses to stay on the shore, but looking to see how deep

---

* The answer, if you're wondering, is several years.

the water is. As I've learned (shamefully slowly) to copy their example, I've found it makes me happier too. I get what I want, and without paying as heavily for it as I often used to.

I've been gullible in the past. Friends have said, 'Come in, the water's lovely! Join us in this business venture/holiday/game'. And I've just jumped in without looking. Funnily enough, sometimes it's turned out that the water is actually cold, murky, muddy, clammy. And invariably wet. Ugh! I've also had friends ask me to support them in ways that I haven't thought through. There's an instinct to help your friends when they're in trouble, but sometimes a loan that isn't repaid is more than you can afford. Or putting in time to listen to their troubles invades so much of your life that your family suffers.

So whether you're jumping off that bridge with a friend or on your own, just check the depth first. The water may indeed be lovely, but sometimes it's better to stand on a bank and dip a toe in, or paddle about a bit, so you have a better idea what it is you're jumping in to.

SOMETIMES IT'S BETTER TO STAND ON A BANK AND DIP A TOE IN, OR PADDLE ABOUT A BIT

RULE 22

Don't dwell on the past

Whatever the past was, it's gone. There is nothing you can do to change anything that has gone before and so you must turn your attention to the here and now. It is hard to resist the allure of dwelling on what has gone before. But if you want to be successful in your life, you have to turn your attention to what is happening for you right now. You might be tempted to dwell on the past because it was awful or because it was wonderful. Either way, you have to leave it behind because the only way to live is in the present.

If you're revisiting the past because of regrets, then you need to be clear that you can't go back and undo what you've done. If you hang on to guilt, you're only damaging yourself. We've all made bad decisions that have adversely affected people around us that we professed to love but whom we treated disgracefully. There isn't anything you can do to wipe the slate clean. What you can do is to resolve not to make such bad decisions again. That's all anyone can ask of us – that we acknowledge where we messed up and are trying our hardest not to repeat the pattern.

If the past was better for you and you hanker after your glory days, then learn to appreciate the memories but also move on and put your efforts into finding a different kind of good time right now. If it truly was better back then (take off those rose-tinted spectacles for a minute), maybe you can analyze exactly why – money, power, health, vitality, fun, youth. Then move on to find other avenues to explore. We all have to leave good stuff behind and find new challenges, new areas to inspire us.

Every day that we wake up to is a fresh start and we can make of it what we want, write what we want on that blank canvas. Keeping that enthusiasm going can be tough – a bit like trying to take up exercise. The first few times are impossibly hard but if you persevere then one day you find you're jogging, walking, swimming without conscious effort. But getting going is really tough and requires immense powers of concentration, enthusiasm, dedication and perseverance to keep at it.

Try to see the past as a room separate from the one you live in now. You can go in there but you don't live there any more. You can go visit but it isn't home any more. Home is here now. Each second of this present is precious. Don't waste any drops of precious time by spending too much time in that old room. Don't miss what is happening now because you were too busy looking back, or later you'll be busy looking back at this time and wondering why you wasted it. Live here, live now, live in this moment.

> LIVE HERE, LIVE NOW,
> LIVE IN THIS MOMENT

Don't live in the future

Blimey, if you thought the previous rule was tough, try this one . . . But the future is where it's all going to happen, I hear you cry. The future is where I'm going to be successful, happy, rich, beautiful, famous, in love, in work, out of this crap relationship, out on the town, surrounded by friends, surrounded by the finest wines money can buy. Yep, those might be plans or dreams or whatever. But again, this here and now is where it is actually at. This is the moment you've been waiting for all your life. This is the moment you must appreciate without all those other things you long for. Look, longing really is the sweetest thing. Having those dreams is brilliant. Don't let anyone ever tell you dreaming is a bad thing. But appreciate that it is the you *right now* that is doing the dreaming. Enjoy the wishing and the longing. Enjoy being alive and having the strength and vitality to do all that dreaming.

Living in the moment doesn't mean throwing away all your responsibilities and cares; it doesn't mean taking off and being a total pleasure seeker; it doesn't mean sitting cross-legged and breathing deeply – although all and any of these things is fine if you want. It just means taking a moment or two every now and then to appreciate being alive and to aim to act like today matters and live life to the full, right here, right now.

We can't project all our future happiness into the future – 'Oh if only I were richer/younger/healthier/happier/more in love/ less in this relationship/had a better job/had nicer children/ had a better car/were slimmer/taller/fitter/had more hair/ better teeth/more clothes' – the list is endless. If only this or that was changed everything would be perfect, wouldn't it? Unfortunately not – it just doesn't work like that. When this and that gets changed there will always be something else, waiting its turn and putting off that happiness until some later date. If you were to suddenly find that you were slimmer/fitter or whatever, then you'd probably find yourself wanting to be richer or that your partner was more loving. You'd find other things to wish for to make you happy.

Forget bigger and better and richer and thinner. The key is to appreciate what we've got right now, and yet still dream and plan. That way we'll be a little happier now than if we're constantly looking to the future, where happiness apparently lies.

And don't go thinking it's all right for me; it's not. I too need to lose a few pounds, certainly get fitter, get more stuff (and how we all love stuff). But I also value the way I am and appreciate what I've got right now because – and this is the secret – it is real. The me that is now is the real me, the future one isn't yet born and may not happen. (You mean I might not lose that extra weight or get fitter? Yep, right.) And the stuff I have now is at least real, tangible, solid. Dreams are great but reality is fine too.

> # DREAMS ARE GREAT BUT
> # REALITY IS FINE TOO

Get on with life – it's whooshing past

Every day, every second, life is whooshing past at an alarming rate. And it goes on getting faster and faster. I once asked an 84-year-old man if life slowed down as you got older. His reply was unprintable but he explained to me in no uncertain terms that no, it didn't. It carried on getting faster. I sometimes wonder if we aren't picking up speed for take-off, if you know what I mean – a sort of run-up before we leave. But the Rule, if you want your life to be successful, happy, fulfilled, meaningful, jam-packed with adventure and reward, is simply to get on with it. And I'm sure you do or you wouldn't be reading this.

So, how do we get on with it? Well, the easiest way is the same way we would get on with anything else we know we have to do. We start with setting a target (a goal, an objective), make a plan, formulate a set of actions to take us towards the target and then, well, get on with it.

Imagine you were a project manager for a big company and they wanted you to organize, say, an exhibition. You would begin with clarifying what you wanted from the exhibition, what it was supposed to achieve (for example, to sell 100 items or to give away free gifts or to drum up 20 new customers). This gives you something to aim for. Then you would formulate your plan – booking the stand, arranging the staff, getting stuff printed, etc. With the plan in place, you would work out what you needed and then get on with it.

Life isn't so different. It's a project – albeit on a vast scale and much more important than an exhibition stand.

I'm sure you get the idea. You have to get on with life, but it is so easy to wallow if you don't have a goal (or goals) and a plan. It's very easy for the days to blur into each other if you've no idea where you are going or what you want to achieve.

None of this, by the way, need take away any spontaneity from life if that's what you're thinking. I don't regard life like a work project, honestly. I do see it as a challenging, rewarding, exciting, rich and diverse, unexpected and rather fantastic experience. But you have to give life a bit of thought if you want to get the best out of it. Without that thought, the days will blur. Without that thought, it's easy to find yourself adrift – floating downstream.

I used to think that whatever turned up would be fine. I was a sort of adventurous fatalist – I would be ready for whatever challenge was thrown my way. But increasingly I see the huge advantage of having a goal and working towards that rather than drifting aimlessly. It makes it so much easier for good things to happen.

> YOU HAVE TO GIVE LIFE A BIT
> OF THOUGHT IF YOU WANT
> TO GET THE BEST OUT OF IT

Be consistent

I had an email from a reader of the first edition of this book, who pointed out that an example I gave in one of the Rules in this book was in breach of another Rule. Nope, I'm not going to tell you which one. You'll have to work it out for yourself like he did.

In my defence, I'd like to point out that this means I *was* following the Rule about not being perfect. However, there's no denying that the reader in question had me bang to rights and, as he observed (very politely I must say), it's important to be consistent.

Well, I've never been arrogant (or stupid) enough to claim that I never break any of the Rules. After all, they're Rules that I know work from observing other people, not a list of personal preferences. So I try to follow them as closely as I can, and the older I get the more often I get it right. But that's not the same as always.

However, we certainly should aim to be consistent about following whatever Rules we decide to live by (the ones in this book and/or any others). There's no point in choosing a path if you're just going to wander off it at whim.

I find that my children are a big help here.* (If you don't have kids you'll have to work that bit harder to identify your own inconsistencies.) If you're debating a point of disagreement with the children (yes, that is indeed a euphemism) you can rely on them to draw your attention to any inconsistencies in your line of argument, or indeed any inconsistencies between what you're telling them now and what you yourself did yesterday. It's a fine line between inconsistency and hypocrisy, and the clearer we are about what we believe and why, the easier it is to be consistent in what we think, say and do.

---

* See! I always knew they'd come in handy for something.

For example, suppose your child points out that you criticize them if they bitch about classmates behind their backs, but you were having a moan about a colleague on the phone to your mum last night. You may need to think about the difference between bitching and having a much-needed moan, and then make sure you're consistent – with yourself as well as your child – about what you allow.

And here's another thing. It makes life easier for everybody else if you are consistent. Erratic people are difficult to live with and be around. So are moody people. If your friends and family don't know how you'll react to the same event or suggestion from one day to the next, you make them live their lives on edge. Unless you are a hermit. I'm not talking about being predictable and boring. Your ideas and activities and enthusiasms can be wonderfully unpredictable and fascinating. It's just your behaviour towards other people that needs to be reliable and consistent. You have the potential to make people's lives richer and easier and better – or darker and trickier and more exhausting. Which do you choose?

> # THERE'S NO POINT IN CHOOSING A PATH IF YOU'RE JUST GOING TO WANDER OFF IT AT WHIM

RULE 26

Dress like today is important

Today is important. Today is the only day you've got that has some reality to it. Why shouldn't you treat it as important? It is. So dress like it matters. And no, I don't mean in the way my mother always used to tell me, 'Make sure you've got clean underwear on; you never know when you'll get run over by a bus'. I loved this as a kid. I couldn't see how important clean underwear would really be when you were lying there in the road. And I used to imagine how, if they got you to the hospital in time and stripped away your torn and blood-soaked trousers, they'd look down and gasp in horror, 'Don't look! This kid has got yesterday's pants on – get him out of here'.

Look, a lot of these Rules are about *conscious* choice, *conscious* decisions, *conscious* awareness. Those I have observed who seem to have got a handle on this thing called life are conscious people. They are awake and aware. They know what they are doing and where they are going. If you too want your life to be more than a set of random events that happen to you and instead make it a series of stimulating challenges and rewarding and enriching experiences, then you too have to be conscious.

And you do this by greeting each day as if it is important. You get up and shower/wash/shave/put on make-up/comb hair/clean teeth etc. and basically do all those things to make you look good, feel good, smell good. And then you dress smartly, cleanly, snappily, stylishly, as if you were going to a job interview or a birthday party or on an outing. If you dress for each day expectantly, importantly, smartly, then each day will become that.

People will react differently to you if you dress as if it matters – and you'll react differently to that different reaction. It's an upward spiral. I have to stress we're not talking formal here, you don't have to be buttoned up and uncomfortable. Just dress as if it matters.

But what about weekends, I hear you ask, surely we can relax then? Of course, but it doesn't mean you should let yourself go. At weekends you're going to see friends and/or family (unless you spend every weekend totally alone) and they too deserve to see you looking good, and as if they matter. Hey, not even your friends want to see you slovenly, dishevelled, untidy, uncared for. But this bit is really about you. If you greet each day as if it is important, then it will do wonders to *your* self-esteem, *your* self-respect, *your* self-confidence.

But, hey, I don't want you taking anything on trust. Try this and see what happens. If you don't perk up and feel completely different within a fortnight, then go back to your old ways and to hell with this Rule. But I can guarantee you'll feel great and face each day livelier and more energetic and happier.

If you adopt the conscious approach to living, you'll find it quite hard to consciously dress down.

PEOPLE WILL REACT
DIFFERENTLY TO YOU IF YOU
DRESS AS IF IT MATTERS

Have a belief system

No, no, no, this isn't where I begin a religious rant or a New Age indoctrination process to welcome you into a strange cult. This is where I simply say that those who have a belief system to sustain them through times of crisis and trouble do better than those who don't. It's that simple.

Now what do we mean by a belief system? Ah, that's harder to put into words. I guess a belief system is what you think the world is all about, the universe and everything. It's what you believe will happen to you after you die. It's what or who you pray to when the night is dark and you are in trouble. Those who have a handle on this curious thing called life seem to be the ones who have worked out, satisfactorily for themselves at least, what they think it's all about. And it doesn't seem to matter what it is they think that is. You could believe in a god or many gods or you could believe in something or someone else – maybe that we're all the product of some weird alien experiment, or you might be a fervent flat earther – it doesn't matter. Well, I guess it will to you, but as long as you have a belief system you will do better than those who don't. Being a seeker is not conducive to having a happy life.

I know you're going to say, 'But what if I haven't been able to find an answer and don't have a belief system? What am I supposed to do then?' Why, carry on looking I guess, but do try to wrap this one up pretty quick as it's an important Rule. Put aside some time to think about it and make sure you put it high on your list of priorities.

I hope you notice I'm not giving you any advice here as to what sort of belief system to have. Any one will do as long as it supports you in times of trouble, answers your questions about your life and what you mean to the universe, and gives you comfort.

You have to be comfortable with your belief system; it's no good having one in which a vengeful and violent deity watches your every move and terrifies you into submission. (Sorry, if you've already got one like that you might need to re-think it.)

You might want to think about whether your belief system makes you feel guilt-ridden or unhappy, asks you to cut bits off your body or in any way mutilate or change your appearance, excludes anyone else on the basis of their race or sex, or needs any formal ritual to bring you the comfort it promises. For some the ideal belief system won't have any sort of figurehead who needs worshipping, obeying or submitting to in any way, shape or form. This is personal, but it's worth thinking about what you are OK with.

A belief system has to be that – a belief. You don't have to prove it to anyone else, justify it, even show it (see Rule 1), convert anyone else to it, or preach to the world in general. You may feel free to take bits from all other belief systems to build your own. But if you can, have something.

> ## YOU DON'T HAVE TO PROVE IT TO ANYONE ELSE, JUSTIFY IT, EVEN SHOW IT

RULE 28

Leave a little space for yourself each day

Most people think they get this but most people might be wrong. You may think you have a little quality time each day for yourself but I bet you don't. You see, even in our time alone we spend so much of it worrying about others, caring for our family, friends and loved ones, that there is very little left over entirely for ourselves. What I am proposing isn't revolutionary or difficult or extreme. In fact it's pretty easy. Just leave a little space for yourself each day. Perhaps only ten minutes (ideally half an hour) put aside and devoted entirely to yourself. Selfish? You bet. Of course it is and justifiably so – you are the captain, the engine, the driving force, the motivator, the rock. You need that time to regenerate, renew, invigorate yourself. You need that down time to recharge and repair. If you don't, you aren't taking on fresh fuel, your engine will run down and so will you.

So what are you going to do with that time? Answer: absolutely nothing. And I do mean nothing. This isn't time for lying in the bath, sitting on the loo, meditating, reading the newspapers, or sleeping. This is a little space for you, a breather, a time to sit still and do absolutely nothing. Just breathe. I find ten minutes sitting in the garden just breathing is a fantastic boost a couple of times a day. I sit there, not thinking, not doing, not worrying, just being, while I appreciate the pleasure of being alive.

I discovered this Rule when I was a teenager. I found it invaluable as a way of purging myself of angst and worries. My mother used to call out to me, 'What are you doing?' to which the reply was inevitably, 'Nothing'. And she would always reply, 'Well, come in here and I'll find you something to do'. She also used to say: 'You'll never amount to anything by having your head stuck in a book'. And the one I loved the most: 'No one needs to think as much as you do'. How do you answer that?

I find time spent doing nothing is really important and as soon as I complicate it, it loses something. If I add a cup of coffee to my solitude, then it's a coffee break and not a space just for me. If I listen to music, then it's a music break. If I have a companion with me and I chat, then it's a social occasion. If I read the papers, then I have moved away entirely from the concept of a little space for me. Keep it simple. Keep it bare. Keep it pure.

> # YOU NEED TIME TO REGENERATE, RENEW, INVIGORATE YOURSELF

Have a plan

You've got to have a plan. A plan is a map, a guide, a target, a focus, a route, a signpost, a direction, a path, a strategy. It says that you are going to go somewhere, do something, be somewhere by a certain time. It gives your life structure and shape, gravitas and power. If you allow life to turn up any old thing you'll be floating downstream as quick as you like. OK, so not all plans work out, not all maps lead to the treasure. But at least you're in with a better chance if you have a map and a shovel than if you just dig at random – or, like most people, don't dig at all.

A plan indicates you've had a bit of a think about your life and aren't just waiting for something to turn up. Or, again like most people, not even thinking about it but going through life perpetually surprised by what happens. Work out what it is you want to do, plan it, work out the steps to take to achieve your goal, and get on with it. If you don't plan your plan, it will remain a dream.

So what happens if you don't have a plan? Well, you reinforce, to yourself, your sense of being 'not in control'. Once you have a plan, everything else falls into place. Once you have a plan, the logical steps to achieve that plan also become available, accessible.

> IF YOU DON'T PLAN
> YOUR PLAN, IT WILL
> REMAIN A DREAM

A plan isn't a dream – it's something you intend doing rather than something you want to do. And having a plan means you've thought through how you're going to do it.

Of course, just because you have a plan doesn't mean that you have to stick to it, to follow it, to obey it to the letter come hell or high water. The plan is always up for review, for improvement, for changing as and when you need to. The plan shouldn't be rigid. Circumstances change, you change, your plan changes. The details of the plan don't matter. Having one does.

Having a plan gives you a fall-back position. When life gets hectic – and boy does it do that sometimes – it is easy to forget what we are here for. Having a plan means that when the dust settles you can remember, 'Now what was I doing? Oh yes, I remember, my plan was to . . .' And off you go again, back on course.

RULE 30

Have a sense of humour

How important this is. As we struggle through this life – and it can be a struggle – we need to keep a sense of proportion about it. What we do and what we take seriously can often be so far removed from what it is actually all about that it is laughable. We get bogged down in trivia, lost in irrelevant detail to such an extent that our life can whizz past and we don't even notice. By letting go of things that really aren't important we can put ourselves back on the right track. And the best way to do that is through humour – laughing at ourselves, laughing at our situation, but never laughing at others; they're just as lost as us and don't need to be laughed at.

We get bogged down with things like worrying what the neighbours will think, concerns over stuff we don't have, or things we haven't done: 'Oh no, I haven't washed the car for two weeks and it's filthy and next door did theirs yesterday so it looks like we are really slovenly'. If we ever think we're getting like that then we do need to have a laugh about it. Life is for living, enjoying the sunshine, big things – not getting in a terrible state because you dropped some eggs on the supermarket floor.

Laughing at yourself and situations you find yourself in has a double positive effect. Firstly, it diffuses tension and helps regain a sense of proportion; and secondly, it has real physical as well as mental benefits. Laughter causes the release of endorphins, which make you feel better as well as giving you a better perspective on life.

This isn't about telling jokes all the time, or cracking witty puns. It's more about being able to see something funny in whatever life throws at us along the way – and there is always some humour in everything. I once came round after being unconscious from a serious car crash. I was in a cubicle in a hospital and in great pain. As I regained consciousness I let out a couple of choice words to describe my condition and, as I did so, the nurse arrived and opened the curtains, only for me to find a nun sat outside.* I was mortified and immediately apologized. She looked at me most gravely, winked, and quietly said, 'It's OK, I've said worse myself'.

If you observe any aspect of human behaviour, you can see the ridiculousness in all of it. Learn to find the funny side of everything. It's the best technique for instant stress relief and dissolves anxiety and doubt. Try it.

> # SEE SOMETHING FUNNY IN WHATEVER LIFE THROWS AT US ALONG THE WAY

---

* Nothing to do with me; she was quietly waiting for another nun who was being checked out for a splinter in her finger, I later discovered.

RULE 31

Choose how you make your bed

Every action you take, every decision you make, everything you do causes an immediate effect on those around you – and on you. And this is the important bit. There *is* such a thing as instant karma. It is your bed and you are going to have to lie in it. Your actions will dictate whether in general your life is going to run happily or badly, smoothly or as if the wheels have fallen off. If you are selfish and manipulative it will rebound on you. If you are generally loving and thoughtful you will get your just rewards – and not in heaven (or the next life or whatever you believe) but right here, right now.

Trust me. Whatever you do and how you do it will come back to you in spades. This isn't a threat, merely an observation. Those who do good, get good. Those who do bad, get bad.

I know we can all point to people who seem to have it made and are still pretty vile. But they don't sleep at night. They have no one to really love them. Inside they are sad and lonely and frightened. Those who go around sharing a bit of love and kindness get rewarded with the same coming back.

It's a bit like the old adage that 'You are what you eat'. You are what you do. Look at the faces of those who spread joy and you will see laughter lines and smiles. Look at those who like to bully and get their own way and are arrogant or demanding or vicious and you will see etched lines of misery and fear, and frowns where there ought to be lightness. These lines won't ever be taken away by face creams or suntans or plastic surgery. They are what they do and you can see it in their eyes. And in the state of their bed, of course.

So be careful how you make your bed. What goes around, comes around. There *is* instant karma. What you sow you reap. Better to stand up and be counted right from the start. Do the right thing, every time. You know what it is. Then when you get in the bed you've made, not only will you be able to sleep at night, but you'll sleep the sleep of the just.

> ## DO THE RIGHT THING, EVERY TIME. YOU KNOW WHAT IT IS

Life can be a bit like advertising

Someone once said that half of the money he spent on advertising was wasted but he didn't know which half.* His point was of course that if you can't tell which half, then you have to keep on doing the whole lot, fully aware that not all of it will produce rewards. Life is a bit like that. Sometimes it seems so unfair. You put in loads of effort and get nothing back. You're polite to people and everyone seems rude back. You work up a sweat and others cruise it. Well, you have to keep on doing the 100 per cent because you don't know which bits will pay off. I know it isn't fair but then life isn't. Your efforts will be rewarded eventually but you'll probably never know which efforts are being rewarded – or for what – and which aren't.

We tend to think we are being lucky sometimes when actually we are just being rewarded for some bit of effort long ago that we have forgotten about. We have to keep going. You can't give up on the grounds that you've had a setback or two because you don't know which setbacks are the ones which count and which ones aren't. I suppose it's like the number of frogs you have to get acquainted with before you find your prince (or princess). Or the pile of oysters you'd have to open to find a pearl.

But whatever you do, don't lose heart because things don't seem to be panning out. Only by keeping up the effort will rewards come in eventually – and you'll never know from which bits comes the best reward.

---

* Lord Leverhulme I believe.

Most well balanced and happy people will tell you that sometimes you have to work at something without looking for a pay-off – apart from the immediate pay-off that we are being kept busy with and thus can't get into trouble. Always looking for success, rewards, a pay-off, can be detrimental to our wellbeing when things don't pan out. Sometimes it's OK to do things just for the sheer enjoyment of doing them. I love painting miniature water-colours – tiny, tiny landscapes. Once in a while someone will come along and suggest I put them into an exhibition or sell them commercially. And every time I do it fails miserably and I give up for a while. Once the dust has settled I always go back to them and I have learnt it is a personal thing and no longer will I try to sell them or show them. They are a not-for-profit part of my life and immensely rewarding. No, you can't see one.

> # YOU'LL NEVER KNOW FROM WHICH BITS OF EFFORT COMES THE BEST REWARD

RULE 33

Get used to stepping outside your comfort zone

Be prepared to be a little bit brave every day. Why? Because if you don't you'll grow stagnant and mouldy or curl up and wither. We all have a comfort zone where we feel safe and warm and dry. But every now and then we need to step outside and be challenged, be frightened, be stimulated. It's this way that we stay young and feel good about ourselves.

If we grow too attached to our comfort zone, chances are it will either start to shrink, or something will come along and dismantle it. Fate, or whatever it is that runs things, doesn't like us to get too complacent and every now and then gives us a great big cosmic kick up the backside to wake us up. If we have practised stretching the boundaries of our woolly cocoon occasionally, that kick won't have too much impact – we're ready for it – it's much easier to cope.

But it's more than that. Expanding your comfort zone makes you feel good about yourself. It gives you extra confidence. And the best bit is that you can do it oh so gently. You don't have to go hang-gliding or fire-walking or have sex with a stranger just to test your comfort zone. It might be as simple as volunteering for something that you've never done before and that you feel slightly nervous about. It could be taking up a new sport or hobby. Maybe it will involve joining something. It could be doing something alone that you've only ever done in company before or speaking up for yourself when you would usually keep quiet.

We impose a lot of restrictions on ourselves that limit us, hold us back. We think we couldn't do that, wouldn't feel happy with that. Taking the challenge of expanding our comfort zone brings us out of ourselves and keeps us learning and growing. You can't grow mould if you're growing experience.

> **EXPANDING YOUR COMFORT ZONE MAKES YOU FEEL GOOD ABOUT YOURSELF**

Learn to ask questions

Look, you may not like the answers but if you ask questions then at least you'll know. Most of the world's problems can be laid firmly at the feet of assumptions. If we assume (no, I'm not going to do that dreadful 'It makes an ass out of u and me' stuff*) then, in effect, we think we know but we don't. We assume that our bit of faulty information is a fact and things go on getting worse. We assume that other people like our plan but they don't and it all goes pear-shaped. Better to ask questions right from the start and know what's what.

Questions help clarify the situation. Questions put people on the spot, which means they have to think – and thinking is always a good thing for everybody about everything. Questions help people clarify their thoughts. Questions demand answers and answers require the situation to be thought through, to its logical conclusion.

As someone very wise and very dear to me once said: 'The better you understand the beliefs, actions, desires and wants of others, the more likely you are to make the right response, alter your own thinking where necessary and generally be successful'.

> ## QUESTIONS HELP PEOPLE
> ## CLARIFY THEIR THOUGHTS

---

* I know I did but that was a joke.

Asking questions gives you time to think, buys you breathing space. Rather than flying off the handle because you think you know the situation, it's better to ask a few questions and find out the truth. You'll be better equipped to respond logically, calmly and correctly.

You can always tell the real Rules Players; they're the ones asking questions while others are reacting, panicking, misinterpreting, assuming, losing control and generally behaving badly.

Ask questions of yourself constantly. Ask why you think you're right – or wrong. Ask yourself why you are doing certain things, want other things, follow a particular course of action. Question yourself firmly and rigorously because maybe there isn't anyone else doing it. And you need it. We all do. It keeps us from assuming we know what's best for ourselves.

And of course there is a time to stop asking questions; of others and of ourselves. You have to know when to back off. All this takes a long time to learn and we all make mistakes as we go. Any questions?

Have dignity

I've spent years watching successful people, and I don't just mean successful as in having lots of money or a big-shot career. In fact one of the most successful people I ever met lived incredibly frugally and simply and reclusively and yet had cracked it in a really big way – happiness, peace, contentment. This was a person you couldn't have wiped the inner smile off even if you had tried.

Almost all successful people have a sense of their own dignity. Now what do I mean by this? Well, they are all pretty solid in themselves; they have worked out who they are and what they are about. They don't need to show off, brag about what they have, or who they are. They don't need to draw attention to themselves because they aren't particularly interested in what we think – they are too busy getting on with things in their own lives. They maintain decorum (lovely old-fashioned word that) not because they are frightened of making a fool of themselves or falling flat on their face but because they simply can't be bothered with attention-seeking stuff.

It is important – if you want to be a successful Rules Player – to show poise, gravitas, be a bit separate from the herd, have good manners, be polite and considerate and to be someone others might like to look up to. You don't have to be all aloof and stand-offish, serious and grown-up. You can still have fun – just don't go making a prat of yourself. You can still let your hair down – just don't let go of control completely. You can still relax – just don't fall off the edge.

Dignity is about showing self-respect and having quiet self-esteem. It's amazing how others will respect you and hold you in greater esteem when you start the ball rolling.

DIGNITY IS ABOUT SHOWING SELF-RESPECT AND HAVING QUIET SELF-ESTEEM

It's OK to feel big emotions

If we're busily maintaining dignity and being peaceful, it's tempting to think that we're detached and so there's no place for big feelings and such like. Well, the good news is, it doesn't work like that. It is OK to feel emotions. It is OK to feel angry when someone really hacks you off. It is OK to feel huge sadness and grief when you lose a loved one. It is OK to feel tremendous joy. It is OK to be scared, anxious, relieved, excited, apprehensive and all the rest.

We are human beings and we have emotions. This is all quite natural. It is quite natural to feel big things deeply and it's OK to let it all show. We don't have to be ashamed of our feelings. It is OK to cry. Sitting on our feelings isn't a good idea. They just get squashed that way. Far better to let them out, deal with them and then get on with things.

If we go through trauma, upsetting experiences and difficult times, it certainly doesn't help to be thinking all the time that we have to keep a lid on it or people will think us weak or out of control. I know it might look as if it contradicts keeping our dignity, but feeling emotion is not undignified unless we express it inappropriately or at the wrong time.

Sometimes even getting angry is totally appropriate – as long as we remain in control and don't do anything we might regret later. Getting angry reminds people that we aren't a pushover and that they have hurt/offended/threatened us deeply and seriously and that their actions have caused us great pain. Of course we shouldn't get angry over silly things – instead we choose to show anger only when it is needed, and needed seriously. Likewise it's not good to get angry and take it out on innocent people – if you can't express the anger appropriately, then you need to find a way of letting it out that isn't going to hurt anybody else. But let it out you must. Bottled anger eats away at you.

It's not just anger that shouldn't be permanently restrained. Neither should fear or anxiety or great joy or any of the other emotions. Just because we are feeling big emotions doesn't mean we are out of control. We can be quite emotional and still be in charge of what we are expressing. You wouldn't be human if you didn't feel stuff – and feel it big time. It is natural and you shouldn't even make any attempt to stifle it. Of course you can make sure it is let out at an appropriate time and place, but that is within your control.

> SITTING ON OUR FEELINGS
> ISN'T A GOOD IDEA.
> THEY JUST GET SQUASHED
> THAT WAY

Keep the faith

... 'We have kept the faith!' we said;
'We shall go down with unreluctant tread.
Rose-crowned into the darkness!'

This is from a poem by Rupert Brooke called *The Hill,* which is about friendship (I think). It may of course be about something entirely different, it's always so hard to tell. But for me it is about the friendship between two lovers, two friends. It is about keeping faith, keeping your promise to support, trust, believe in. It may of course be about keeping faith as a religious thing, but knowing Brooke's poems I somehow don't think so.

Keeping the faith is about sticking to your promises, going down into darkness rose-crowned, proud, unreluctant, knowing you've done the right thing, stuck by your friends in times of trouble. These are perhaps old-fashioned values – honour, loyalty, trust, pride, support, fidelity, reliability, dependability, strength, seeing things through, constancy – but no less worth having for all that. We live in a throw-away society and keeping your word, being there when you said you would, being dependable and reliable, makes you stand out as a person of some value, some worth. This is a good thing.

We fight shy of being 'good' these days in case people mistake us for 'goody-goodies'. But that's another thing entirely. Keeping the faith is something you do. Being a goody-goody is when you try to convert others. Having your own values and keeping them to yourself (sticking to Rule 1) is fine. Trying to make everyone else do the same as you is a bad thing. That makes you a goody-goody.

No, it doesn't apply to me because I'm only giving out information, not trying to convert you. It is entirely up to you whether you pick up this information and run with it. But I can guarantee you I shall keep the faith and the information I give you today will be the same information I would give you in 20 years' time. Old-fashioned values don't ever go out of style (perhaps they've always been out) and I shan't let you down.

KEEPING THE FAITH IS SOMETHING YOU DO. BEING A GOODY-GOODY IS WHEN YOU TRY TO CONVERT OTHERS

Here's another bit from the same poem:

> . . . Proud we were,
> And laughed, that had such brave true things to say.

You'll never understand everything

Look, we are tiny complex humans in a huge complex world (and even bigger universe). It's all so unimaginably, fantastically strange that, believe me, we'll never be able to understand everything. And that applies at all levels and in all areas of life. Once you grasp this Rule you'll sleep easier at night.

There are likely to be a few things going on around you right now, as there always will be, that will remain just slightly outside your comprehension. People will behave oddly and you won't understand why. Things will go unexpectedly wrong – or right – and it won't make sense. Spend all your time desperately trying to work it all out and you'll drive yourself crazy. Much better just to accept that there is always stuff that we won't understand and let it go at that. How simple that is.

> **PEOPLE WILL BEHAVE ODDLY. THINGS WILL GO UNEXPECTEDLY WRONG – OR RIGHT**

It's the same principle for the big stuff – why things happen to us, why we are here, where we go afterwards, that sort of thing. Some of it we'll never know, some of it we can try and work out, but I have a sneaking feeling it won't turn out to be anything like we think.

It's as if our lives are an enormous jigsaw and all we get access to is the bottom left-hand bit. And from that we make these huge assumptions: 'Oh, it's a . . .' But when the veil gets taken away we see that the jigsaw is massive and that the one tiny bit we were scrutinizing was actually something else, and there we are looking at an entirely different picture to the one we'd imagined.

We are now collecting information faster than any human, or any computer, can process it. We can't understand it all. We can't even begin to understand a tiny fraction of it. Same with our lives. Stuff is going on around us at such a rate we'll never get to the bottom of it. Because as fast as we try, the picture changes, new information comes in and our understanding alters.

Be curious, ask questions, wonder to yourself, talk to other people if you like – but know that this won't always give you a clear and concrete answer. People don't always make sense. Life doesn't always make sense. Let it go and discover the peace of mind that comes with knowing that you'll never understand everything. Sometimes it just is.

Know where true happiness comes from

No, I'm not about to reveal the secret people have sought since the beginning of time – where true happiness comes from. But I do know where it *isn't* to be found. And I do have an inkling where it might be. Let's take a scenario. You go out to buy a new car/house/suit/computer/whatever turns you on. You have the money (no, I have no idea where you get it from, this is just an example) and you buy whatever it is, and it makes you feel incredible/happy/excited/fantastic. Now imagine whoever it was who built/made/created whatever it is you bought. When they made it, where did they fit that feeling in? I think you might have brought that feeling with you.

Now imagine you fall in love. It is, again, incredible. You feel fantastic, happy, excited. You go to meet your new love and, when you see them, that feeling spills out in all directions. You feel amazing because you are with them and they are generating that feeling. Right? Wrong. Again you brought it all with you. You may look to them to trigger it but even if they go to the other end of the planet, you'll still have that feeling and they're nowhere near you.

> I THINK YOU MIGHT HAVE BROUGHT THAT FEELING WITH YOU

You get fired. Ghastly. You get given your papers. You walk away devastated. You feel like nothing. Where in that documentation is that feeling you now have? Nowhere, that's right. Again you brought it all with you. We all go to work every day with the potential to have that 'I've just been fired' feeling. We all meet new people with the 'I've fallen head over heels in love' feeling.

But no amount of falling in love, buying new stuff or getting sacked is going to keep that feeling going for longer than it takes us to get over it. People get addicted to buying new stuff or falling in love or whatever because they just love that feeling without realizing that they already have it. They have to keep having their 'fix' because they think it's the only way to get that feeling going. The secret is knowing how to trigger it without anyone else or anything else being involved. No, I don't know. You have to find that one for yourself. Clue: it's the one place you'd never think of looking. Yep, right inside you.

Life is a pizza

I love my kids. I love reading to them, playing with them, watching them grow up, listening to them talk, teaching them to ride bikes, taking them to the beach, and generally hanging out with them.

Mind you, I hate picking up after them, listening to them squabble, and being spoken to in that dismissive way that only teenagers can really do justice to. But I can't seem to have the good bits without the picking up, the squabbles and the sharp end of a teenager's tongue from time to time. I wouldn't be without them though (most days).

I love pizza too. I love crispy pizzas and I like the soft squishy ones. Any pizza really. I love pepperoni and mozzarella and tomatoes and juicy chunks of ham and piquant capers and crispy onions. Mind you, I hate olives, and they sometimes appear on pizzas without being ordered. Disgraceful. And those dried up tomatoes you sometimes get. The ones that are all chewy. Ugh! I always pick those off and throw them away.

When my kids were little they'd refuse to eat a pizza that had something they didn't like on it. They'd burst into tears and sob, 'I hate mushrooms!' or 'I can't stand cooked tomatoes!' They had to learn that if they couldn't work round the mushrooms or cooked tomatoes, they couldn't have pizza at all.

You know what I'm going to say. Yes, life is a pizza, with everything on it. If you want the good bits you have to deal with the bad bits. If you love everything about your job apart from the one person you don't like dealing with, recognize that the job comes as a package and you buy into it or jack the job. If you love your partner but hate the way they sulk after a row, accept them as they are and recognize that the sulking is the bit that reminds you of how wonderful everything else is. If your neighbour is friendly and keeps an eye on your property when you're out and signs for your deliveries and babysits the kids, you just have to live with the fact that she talks too much and stop moaning about it. And when you stop moaning, you'll probably find you mind it much less.

I know parents who move their child from school to school until they find one that's perfect in every way. They never do of course, but eventually they have to stop because the child has grown up. I'm not saying you should never move your child (if you have the option) but stop looking for perfection because you won't find it. Life isn't perfect. Nothing in life is perfect.

The best things in life come with chewy dried tomatoes and olives. There's no point moaning. Just pick them off, or swallow them down as fast as you can, and then sink your teeth into what's left and relish every bite.

> # THE BEST THINGS IN LIFE COME WITH CHEWY DRIED TOMATOES

Always have someone – or something – that is pleased to see you

I know a woman with greyhounds (see Rule 55). When she comes home her dogs are always pleased to see her, but then dogs always are. No matter how badly you have treated them* they always go nuts. Of course, you want your partner to behave in just the same fashion, to go nuts when you come home. And I'm sure they do, don't they? And of course you do when they come home, don't you? No? Why not? Yes? Well done.

We all need someone who is pleased to see us. It makes us feel it is all worthwhile. I love it when I have to go away for work for a day or two and then when I get back my children all stand there, like children do, with their hands outstretched with that lovely, 'Have you brought me something back?' look on their faces.

Or when they get back from school and you ask if they've had a good day and they grunt at you. So refreshing. But you are still incredibly pleased to see them – for them you are their someone or something.

And no, the red light of the TV standby button isn't enough. You do need a person or a pet. One of my sons claims his gecko is always pleased to see him but I have tried hard to detect any emotion on its face and so far failed – the gecko's not my son's.

---

* Not taking them on a long enough walk because you've been so busy, forgetting biscuits, stuff like that. I don't mean treating them really badly; who would do that?

> # WE ALL NEED SOMEONE WHO IS PLEASED TO SEE US. IT MAKES US FEEL IT IS ALL WORTHWHILE

Having someone or something who is pleased to see you is important because it gives you someone who needs you and this gives you a purpose, stops you getting self-absorbed, gives you a reason for getting on with life. But what if you live alone and don't have pets or children? Well, voluntary or charity work is a very good way to quickly get in the situation where somebody is pleased to see you. Then again, it could be right on your doorstep.

Even living alone in a part of London where nobody really talked to their neighbours, a friend of mine discovered there was a retired disabled man who lived a few doors down from her. She noticed that he found excuses to 'just happen to be at his door' as she walked past on her way back from work most days. He was clearly a bit lonely and really valued a quick chat (or a longer one if possible). He was pleased to see her. Who is pleased to see you?

Know when to let go – when to walk away

Sometimes you have to just walk away. We all hate to fail, hate to give up, hate to give in. We love the challenge of life and want to keep on until whatever we are trying to 'win' has been overcome, vanquished, beaten, won. But sometimes it just ain't going to happen and we need to learn to recognize those moments, learn how to shrug philosophically and walk away with our pride intact and our dignity high.

Sometimes you really want to do something, but it is unrealistic. Instead of knocking yourself out, cultivate the art of knowing when to walk away and you'll find it a lot less stressful.

If a relationship is coming to its end, instead of playing out long and complicated – and potentially hurtful – end games, learn the art of walking away. If it's dead, leave it. This isn't a Rule that should be in the partnership section – it's here because it is for you, to protect you, to nurture you. This is nothing to do with 'them' but all to do with you. If it's dead, don't go digging it up every five minutes to check if there's a pulse. It's dead, walk away.

You may want to get even – don't get mad, walk away. This is much better than getting even because it shows you have risen above whatever it is that is driving you crazy. And there can be no better way of getting even than to ignore something so completely it can be left behind.

Letting go and walking away means you are exercising control and good decision-making powers – you are making your choice rather than letting the situation control you.

> # IF IT'S DEAD, DON'T GO DIGGING IT UP EVERY FIVE MINUTES TO CHECK IF THERE'S A PULSE. IT'S DEAD, WALK AWAY

I don't want to be rude but your problems – hey, my problems too – won't even warrant a footnote in the history of the universe. Walk away now and look back after ten years and I bet you'll be hard pushed to even remember what it was all about. No, this isn't a 'time is the best healer' crusade, but putting space and time between you and your troubles does give you a wider view, a better perspective. And the way to do that is to walk away, put that space there. Time will put itself there, in time of course.

Retaliation leads to escalation

Now I'll be honest here. Among my friends I'm not actually known for my tolerance or my ability to let things lie. Frankly, if someone puts me down or winds me up, my first instinct is to respond in kind. When I was (much) younger this led to the occasional fist fight. Even when I learnt to stop picking fights – or letting other people pick them with me – I still couldn't resist a smartass retort or a petty act of vengeance.

Well, it's hard. If your neighbour cuts down a tree that's technically yours, you feel aggrieved and want to cut down one of their trees that overhangs your fence. Even if you didn't particularly like the original tree – which isn't the point. Or perhaps a colleague at work takes credit for an idea that you came up with. How tempting to get back at them by omitting to mention until the last minute that the deadline on their current project is being brought forward, or by drawing attention to the fact that last month's catastrophic exhibition was their idea.

However, think about it. After many years even I learnt to think this one through, so I'm sure you can. Anyone who is prepared to cut down your tree or nick your idea isn't about to take your little act of revenge lying down. Nope. They're going to bulldoze your garage next, or try to get you fired. Then what'll you do? Blow up their car? Hire an employment lawyer? Are you sure this isn't getting out of hand?

Actually this is one lesson I learnt from my kids.* The thing about siblings is that they're so upfront with their squabbles that you can watch the whole thing spiral out of control much faster than in grown-up versions. We so-called adults plot and

---

* And I've been trying to teach it back to them ever since.

scheme and plan our Machiavellian strategies over days or even months.

Brothers and sisters can go from a minor disagreement to all-out war within minutes.

Look, retaliation can only lead to one thing – an escalation of hostilities. That's the story of wars the world over and throughout history. And we're no different in our dealings with neighbours, colleagues and all those other people we get thrown together with, whether we like them or not.

So how do we call an end to this madness? The cycle is only broken when one of those involved is mature enough to see that someone has got to bite their tongue, or hold back, in order to stop it in its tracks. Someone has to be grown-up enough to bite their tongue, assume the moral high ground, take it like a man,* call a halt and just let the whole thing drop. Yes, even when you have got a really cutting retort, or cunning masterstroke, up your sleeve. It really is sometimes better to do nothing, say nothing. Come on, if I can do it, anyone can.

> ## IT REALLY IS SOMETIMES BETTER TO DO NOTHING, SAY NOTHING

---

* Or woman, of course.

Look after yourself

You are the boss, the captain, the driving force. If you are sick, who is going to run the ship? There is no one else. It makes sense to look after yourself. And I have no intention of getting all preachy here and telling you to go to bed early, eat your greens and take loads of exercise – that would all be pure hypocrisy because I don't do any of those things. Doesn't mean you shouldn't, however. They are all good ideas.

An occasional quick body service might be a good idea, a regular check-up to nip any potential problems in the bud. I have an annual one. I would also suggest that some foods are like dynamite and they fill you with energy, speed your metabolism and make you feel great. Other foods make you sluggish, get stored as fat and slow you down. They might also do you long-term damage in the way of clogging up bits. Now the choice is entirely yours but the machine that is you runs better on high-energy food and worse on junk food.

Same with sleep. Going without makes you tired. Having too much makes you lethargic. Getting the right amount makes you feel good. Going back to sleep makes you feel blurry. Getting up straight away makes you feel good – and noble. Nothing better. But of course all this is entirely up to you. No one is going to stand behind you any more and make sure you've washed behind your ears or check your shoes are clean and polished. You're a grown-up and on your own now. Fantastic. But it means you have all the responsibility too.

Rules Players eat well, sleep well, relax a lot, take exercise (and no, computer games don't count). They also stay away from potentially harmful situations. They know how to stay out of danger, avoid threatening encounters and generally take care of themselves.

YOU'RE A GROWN-UP AND ON YOUR OWN NOW

Looking after yourself is exactly that. Not relying on anyone else to make sure you are fed on time and fed well, washed and ready to go, comfortable, tidy, healthy and let out regularly for your walk. It's great being a grown-up. You get to stay up all night partying if you want to, but you can also choose to take care of yourself if you want to.

Maintain good manners in all things

In her wonderful book *Watching the English,** Kate Fox observes that in any small transaction, like buying a newspaper, there will be around three pleases and two thank-yous – and that's a minimum. Yes, the English (and a few other nationalities besides) are terribly polite but what's wrong with that? We have to interact with a whole host of people every day and a little politeness has to be a good thing. The Rules Player maintains good manners in all things. And if you don't know what good manners are, then we are in trouble.

You're probably thinking that you have good manners already. Most of us believe we do. However, the more you hurry and the more stress you are under, the more manners are likely to slip. All of us, if we're honest, will admit to forgetting to properly express gratitude for something when frazzled by life, or feeling a huge temptation to push in front of somebody doddery when rushing to catch a train.

However rushed and fraught you are (and following the Rules should make you less so), you should always make the effort to show these good manners:

- queuing without jostling
- complimenting people when you need to (and when they deserve it, no use throwing compliments around if they aren't justified and earned)
- not sticking your nose in where it isn't wanted
- keeping a promise

---

* *Watching the English: The Hidden Rules of English Behaviour* by Kate Fox (Hodder & Stoughton, 2004).

- keeping a secret
- keeping basic table etiquette (oh come on, you know this stuff: no elbows, no talking with your mouth open, no over-stuffing your mouth, no flicking peas with your knife)
- not shouting at people who get in your way
- apologizing when you get in someone else's
- being civil
- not swearing or being religiously profane
- opening the door ahead of people
- standing back when there's a rush
- answering when spoken to
- saying 'Good morning' and such like
- thanking people when they've looked after you or done something for you
- being hospitable
- observing manners of other communities
- not grabbing the last piece of cake
- being courteous and charming
- offering visitors refreshment and going to the front door to say goodbye to them.

No matter how many small interactions with people you have each day, don't let the manners slip. They cost nothing and yet can generate so much good will and make everyone's life that much more pleasant.

A LITTLE POLITENESS HAS
TO BE A GOOD THING

Prune your stuff frequently

Why? Because collecting clutter clutters your home, your life and your mind. A cluttered home is symbolic of cluttered thinking. Rules Players are clear and direct in their thinking and don't collect junk. If only. We all do of course. All I am suggesting is that occasionally clearing some of it out might be a good idea before it overwhelms you emotionally and gets more and more cobwebby.

Pruning your stuff gives you a chance to get rid of anything that is useless, broken, out of date, un-cool, un-cleanable, redundant and ugly. It was, after all, William Morris who said not to have anything in your home that wasn't useful or beautiful. Having a good clear-out refreshes you, revitalizes you, makes you conscious of what you are collecting – and anything that makes us conscious is a good thing in my book.

Again, I have noticed a difference between successful people and those who seem to labour in a backwater never really getting their lives off the ground. Those who are punchy and getting on with things are also those who have an amazing ability to prune stuff, clear the clutter, sort the wheat from the chaff. Those who are having trouble getting lift-off are those running along the tarmac still clutching black plastic sacks full of useless stuff they bought from the charity shop and have never thrown away – or never opened since they bought them. They have cupboards full of junk that is just taking up space, drawers full of broken things and wardrobes full of clothes they can no longer get into or which have so long gone out of fashion they may be worth something as collector's items but will never be worn again.

There is an 'unburdening' effect that comes with pruning. You have more space in your home, a feeling of being more in control, and you get rid of that slightly overwhelmed feeling that comes with having piles of stuff accumulating everywhere. You don't have to live in a spotless house full of designer furniture and minimalist styling. All I'm suggesting is that if you want to find out what's holding you back, try looking in the cupboard under the sink or under the bed or on top of the wardrobe in the spare room.

> # CLUTTER OVERWHELMS YOU EMOTIONALLY AND GETS MORE AND MORE COBWEBBY

Remember to touch base

Before you can touch base you have to know where base is. Base is home. Base is where you belong. Base is where you feel comfortable, secure, loved, restored and trusted. Base is where you feel strong and in control. Base is anywhere you can kick your shoes off, metaphorically and physically, and rest your head safe in the knowledge you'll be looked after.

We all lead increasingly busy, frenetic and frantic lives. We all get caught up in the hurly-burly of life to such an extent that we lose sight of where we thought we were going and what we thought we were going to do and what we were going to achieve. Base is going back to where you dreamed it all, planned it all out. Base is where you were before you got lost.

Base camp might well be rediscovering our roots – essential in an age when we all move around so much. Knowing who your family is, where you come from, what your real background is. It's OK to have ambition and move on from our roots, but it's also important to know who we are and where we came from. You can sometimes sense it in celebrities who have become incredibly famous or rich. Often they try to deny their past and pretend to be something else and in the process they come across as shallow and fake.

> **BASE IS WHERE YOU WERE**
>
> **BEFORE YOU GOT LOST**

For you, base might be a place where you grew up, where you're reminded of the feelings of growing up – the hopes and fears, the younger you. Or it might be a person who provides the base – a best friend from many years ago who can remind you of how you were before it all got so confusing.

Of course, we might not all know where we come from and we have to make allowances for that. You might be adopted, but you were raised somewhere. Whatever your circumstances, you will have something that makes you feel grounded if you look for it. It doesn't have to be where you were born and raised. If you are really struggling, then it's possible to create yourself a new base. Anywhere that makes you feel secure is fine.

We all need time with people or in places where we can be ourselves, where we don't have to explain, justify, provide background or give a good impression. That's the joy of touching base – being somewhere where you are accepted without question and everything around you reminds you of what's really important. Touching base is something that, when we do it, we wonder why on earth we left it so long.

Draw the lines around yourself

Personal boundaries are the imaginary lines you draw around yourself that no one should cross either physically – unless invited in – or emotionally. You are entitled to respect, privacy, decency, kindness, love, truth and honour, to name but a few rights. If people cross the lines, blur the boundaries, you are entitled to stand up for yourself and say, 'No, I won't put up with this'.

But you have to draw the lines first. You have to know what you will stand for and what you won't. You have to set the boundaries in your own mind before you can expect others to respect them, stick to them.

The more secure you become with your boundaries, the less power other people will have over you. The more clearly defined your boundaries, the more you realize that other people's stuff is more to do with them and less to do with you – you stop taking things so personally.

You are entitled to basic self-respect. You can't expect others to respect you unless you respect yourself. You can't respect yourself until you have formed a clear picture of who you are and what you are. And setting boundaries is part of this process. You have to feel important enough to set those lines. And once set, you have to be assertive enough to reinforce them.

Setting personal boundaries means you don't have to be scared of other people any more. You now have a clear idea of what you will put up with and what you won't. Once someone crosses the line between appropriate and inappropriate behaviour, it gets really easy to say, 'No, I don't want to be treated like this/spoken to like this'.

SETTING PERSONAL BOUNDARIES MEANS YOU DON'T HAVE TO BE SCARED OF OTHER PEOPLE ANY MORE

Probably the best way to start this is with your own family. Over the years we get set in patterns of behaviour. Say, for example, you are used to going to visit your parents and coming away feeling bad because they put you down or made you feel inadequate. You can change things by saying to yourself, 'I won't put up with this any more'. And then don't put up with it. Speak your mind. Say you don't like being criticized/told off/made to feel small – you are an adult now and entitled to respect and encouragement.

Setting personal boundaries enables us to resist pushy people, rude people, aggressive people, people who would take advantage of us, people who would use us unwisely and unwell. Successful people know their worth and don't get messed around. Successful people are the ones who can recognize emotional blackmail, people playing games with them, people on the make, people who themselves are weak and needy, people who dump on others, people who need to make you look small to make themselves feel big. Once you've got those lines drawn around you, it gets a whole lot easier to stay behind them and be firm, resolute, strong and assertive.

Shop for quality, not price

I have to admit my wife taught me this one, for which I am eternally in her debt. To me it seemed a natural thing to shop for price. Perhaps this is what chaps do. I would work out what I wanted and then go and buy the cheapest items I could and feel really pleased with myself for saving money. And then I was always dissatisfied with what I had. Stuff broke or didn't work or wore out quickly or looked shoddy after a very short time. I was living in a mess – and a cheap one at that. What I needed to learn was the art of quality shopping.

Basically:

* Accept only the very best – second best is not for you, ever.

* If you can't afford it, don't buy it, *or* wait and save until you can.

* If you have to have it, buy the very best you can afford.

There, that's pretty easy, isn't it? Well, for me it wasn't as easy as that. It took me quite a long time to really get to grips with this one. It isn't that I don't – or didn't then – admire quality or appreciate excellence; it was that I was impulsive. If I thought I needed something, I wanted it right then and there. And if I couldn't afford the very best, I would settle for the cheapest. In fact, in a very English sort of way, I thought that 'getting a bargain' was what it was all about. We don't like to talk about money and we don't like to brag about how much something cost, too tacky by far – better to buy tacky in the first place. I think not.

IF YOU CAN'T AFFORD IT, DON'T BUY IT

Going for quality doesn't mean we're stuck up or a load of toffs or living beyond our means. Going for quality means you appreciate the finer things, can see the sense in buying well-made, well-produced things, as they will:

- last longer

- be stronger

- not break so easily.

And this means they will not need to be replaced so often, which means you might actually be saving money. They will also make you look and feel better.

Now that I've latched on to this Rule I really enjoy that anticipation before I buy something. I make sure it really is the quality I am going for and not just the price. I still shop around for a bargain though – it's just now I look for the quality items but I'm prepared to find them at the lowest price.

It's OK to worry, or to know how not to

The future is uncertain, scary, hidden. We wouldn't be human if we didn't worry about things at times. We worry about our health, our parents/kids/friends, our relationships, our work and our spending. We worry that we are getting older, fatter, poorer, more tired, less attractive, less fit, less mentally alert, less everything really. We worry about things that matter and things that don't. Sometimes we worry about not worrying.

Look, it really is OK to worry. Just so long as there is something real to worry about. If there isn't, then all you're doing is putting wrinkles in your brow – and that makes you look older you know.

The first step is to decide whether there is something you can do about whatever it is you are worrying about, or not. There are usually logical steps to take to eliminate that worry. I worry that people aren't taking those steps, which means they are choosing to hang on to their worries rather than be free of them.

If you are worried then:

- get practical advice
- get up-to-date information
- do something, anything, as long as it is constructive.

If you are worrying about your health, go and see a doctor. If you are worrying about money, set a budget and spend wisely. If you are worrying about your weight, go to the gym, eat less, do more. If you are worrying about a lost kitten, phone the vet/ police/local animal rescue. If you are worrying about getting older, there is simply no point – it's happening whether you worry or not.

> ALL YOU ARE DOING IS
> PUTTING WRINKLES IN
> YOUR BROW – AND THAT
> MAKES YOU LOOK OLDER
> YOU KNOW

If there is nothing you can do about your worry (or if you are a persistent worrier, even bordering on the neurotic), then distraction is the only answer. Get absorbed in something else. A man with the rather impressive name of Mikhail Csikszentmihalyi identified something called 'flow', where you are so absorbed in a task you are doing, so fully immersed, that you become almost unaware of external events. It's a pleasurable experience and it completely banishes worry. He also said: 'The quality of our lives improves immensely when there is at least one other person who is willing to listen to our troubles.'

Worrying may be a symptom that you don't really want to *do* something about the problem. It might be easier just to carry on worrying – or look concerned and appear to worry – rather than do something about it. It is OK to worry properly, profitably, usefully. It is not OK to worry pointlessly or needlessly. Or at least, it is OK but it's a colossal waste of life.

Stay young

I did say earlier that if you were worrying about getting older, you should stop as there wasn't anything you could do about it. It's inevitable. So why a Rule saying 'Stay young'? Well, growing older physically (and temporally) is something we all have to do and putting it off by endless surgery and the like is pointless. Better to stay young. And by this I mean mentally and emotionally. Billy Connolly made a wry observation in one of his shows when he bent down to pick something up and made a noise, a sort of bending grunt that oldies make. And he said he didn't know when he had started to make that noise but it had crept up on him and he made it now. That's what I'm talking about – all those noises and actions we make to indicate we're old. All that wrapping up well when we go out in case we catch a chill. All that making sure we take our coat off when we come in, even if we're going straight out again, or we won't feel the benefit. All that 'I'd rather just have a cup of tea if it's all right with you' stuff. All that 'We're going to the same place we always go on holiday – you know what you're getting'.

I was reading yesterday about a chap who had just taken his father backpacking in the Greek islands. His dad is aged 78 and he said he had trouble keeping up with him. Now that's staying young. I know a woman in her sixties who describes how she feels the same inside now as she did when she was 21. And it shows outside. That's staying young.

Staying young is trying new things, not grumbling or saying all the things you know people say as they get older. It's not going for the safe option; it's staying abreast of what is happening; not giving up stuff like cycling because you think you're too old for it. (If you are very young, by the way, I do apologize for all this but you will need it one day, believe me.)

Staying young is trying out new tastes, new places to go, new styles, keeping an open mind, not getting reactionary (hmmm, I should read this again) or being disapproving of more and more things, not settling for what you've always had or always done. Staying young is about keeping a fresh vision of the world, being interested, being stimulated, being motivated, being adventurous.

Staying young is a state of mind.

> # STAYING YOUNG IS TRYING OUT NEW TASTES, NEW PLACES TO GO, NEW STYLES

RULE 52

Throwing money at a problem doesn't always work

Years ago when I worked in one particular industry, whenever something was going wrong my boss would always sigh and say, 'Well, I guess we can try the "American solution"'.* What he meant, basically, was throw money at it until it went away. At work this approach often works wonders but problems in life tend to need a more hands-on approach, a more delicate touch. We tend to think that if we just chuck enough money at things they'll get sorted out, instead of finding ways to really sort them out that require time and attention and care.

Let's go back to that getting older thing again. You might think that throwing money at it in the shape of cosmetic surgery might be the answer but it isn't; it only delays things and can create worse problems than it solves. How much better to work on one's mental approach to ageing and come to terms with it in a dignified and graceful way instead. If somebody you care about seems distracted, tense, not themselves, then buying them a present might well cheer them up, but the better (and cheaper) option is to make time to take them out for a walk and ask them about themselves, giving them the opportunity to talk.

We tend to think that if we spend more money on something it will solve the problem. Maybe sometimes we need an old-fashioned approach of time and attention and finding out.

---

* This in no way is meant to be derogatory towards Americans or their solutions. Look, it works. I have no gripe with this method at work, it's just that in our personal life it isn't so efficient, but I don't mean to be rude.

Like our grandparents, who didn't throw something away and get a new one when it had stopped working – they patiently sat down and tried to sort out what it was that had gone wrong and if there was a way to put it right again. That went for relationships as well as for watches or kettles.

Throwing money at things makes us feel powerful and grown-up when instead we might need to stand back and see if we couldn't do better by changing the situation another way. I know I'm as guilty of this one as anybody. It happens to me most with cars. I buy a car – usually an expensive, temperamental, costly-to-fix model. Then when it goes wrong, as it invariably does, I pay the garage to come out and take it away and spend a fortune having it put right. How much simpler my life would be if I could stand back and see that the car was unsuitable in the first place, basically a mistake. Throwing money at it now doesn't alleviate the problem, it merely delays it, puts it off until the next time when it goes wrong again. And it will. Oh believe me, it will, it always does. In this case the American solution most definitely doesn't work.

> # THROWING MONEY AT IT DOESN'T ALLEVIATE THE PROBLEM, IT MERELY DELAYS IT

Think for yourself

You'll think this one's so obvious you'll be wondering what it's doing in here and I do apologize if it seems patronizing, simplistic or downright rude. I don't mean to offend or insult and I do appreciate that you do think for yourself. I guess what I mean by this Rule is that we need to be incredibly clear about our opinions, grounded in our own sense of identity, and very assertive about being *us* so that we aren't easily swayed by what other people think of us. It's tougher than it looks at first glance. We are all vulnerable inside. We all have fears and concerns. We all want to be loved and accepted. We all want to blend in, be one of a crowd, be acknowledged. We all want to belong. The temptation is to say 'I'll be whatever you want me to be'.

Being original or creative or different can make us think we stand out too much and will get shunned. But truly successful people aren't shunned, instead they become pack leaders because of their originality, their difference. If you are obnoxious or rude or hurtful, you will indeed be shunned. But if you are kind, thoughtful, caring and respectful you will be loved and accepted. If you are also original in your thinking, you will be looked up to, respected and admired.

To think for yourself you have to be pretty sure of who you are and be clear in your thinking as well as doing it for yourself – there's no point in thinking for yourself if it's all muddled and woolly.

I have a friend who is very intelligent and astute but all her opinions come from reading a particular national newspaper. Whatever line it takes on a particular issue is the same line she will come out with. She trusts her paper implicitly and is unable to see how predictable her views are – seeing as they are always based on what she has read. She will argue her case articulately, forcefully and in a well-reasoned way, but always absolutely in line with her paper's views. Sometimes we can all be a bit like that and need to change where we get our information from occasionally to make sure we stay fresh and original.

Of course, to think for yourself means you have to (a) have something to think about and (b) actually do the thinking. Look at a selection of people you know. If they are at one with their own life, I bet they are doing both. If they are badly adjusted and generally struggling, I bet they're not doing either.

> WE ALL WANT TO BLEND IN, BE ONE OF A CROWD, BE ACKNOWLEDGED. WE ALL WANT TO BELONG

You are not in charge

Sorry if this comes as a shock but you're not in charge – no matter how much you want to be, no matter how much you think you are, no matter how much you deserve to be. If you are not in charge, it doesn't mean anybody else is either. We may all be on the same runaway train with no driver or there may indeed be a driver (the driver may be insane, drunk or asleep but that's another thing entirely).

Once you accept that you are not in charge, you can let go of so much stuff. It's very liberating. Instead of complaining, 'Why isn't it like this?' you can accept it isn't and let it go. Instead of metaphorically bashing your head against a metaphoric brick wall, you can walk away whistling with your hands in your pockets – you are, after all, not in charge and therefore not responsible.

Once you get your head around the wonderful concept that you are here to enjoy and not here to run things, then you are free to sit in the sunshine a bit more often, take time off.

Look, stuff happens. Good stuff and bad stuff. There may or there may not be a driver. You can blame the driver if you want. You can accept that if there isn't a driver, the journey will sometimes be scary, sometimes exhilarating, sometimes boring, sometimes beautiful (actually whether there is or isn't a driver the same holds true). We have to have both the good stuff and the bad stuff. That's a fact. If you or I were in charge, we'd probably interfere too much and get rid of most of the bad stuff and the human race would die out ever so quickly due to stagnation, lack of challenge, lack of motivation and lack of excitement. It is, after all, the bad stuff that fires us up, makes us learn and gives us a reason for living. If it was all good it would be awfully fluffy and boring.

A slight condition to this one, though. You might not be running the show but that doesn't discharge you of all responsibilities. You still have obligations – you still need to be respectful of the world you live in and the people you live in it with – it's just that you don't have overall responsibility for the whole show and everything in it.

Seeing as you are not in charge you can watch it like a movie and cheer at the exciting bits, cry at the sad bits and hide during the scary moments. But you are not the director or even the projectionist. You are not even the usherette.* You are the audience. Enjoy the show.

> ## ONCE YOU ACCEPT THAT YOU ARE NOT IN CHARGE, YOU CAN LET GO

---

* There's probably a frightfully modern PC word for this job. Please don't write in.

RULE 55

Have something in your life that takes you out of yourself

I have a friend who swears by her adopted greyhounds. No, I don't mean she stands next to them and curses, although I'm sure she does from time to time. But what I mean is that no matter how miserable she is, no matter how hard she's been working, no matter how annoying life has been, no matter how fed up, cross, or what sort of a bad hair day she's had, when she gets home and gets that incredible greeting from her rescued dogs it all then becomes worthwhile. The gloom is lifted and she is instantly restored, calm, happy and loved. It's a bit sad but there you go (only joking).

For me it has to be my children and where I live. Although my kids drive me insane at times, there is still something incredibly magical about the way they view the world and how they grow. As for where I live, I only have to think about going home to feel lifted and invigorated.

For every one of us there will be something different that does it, that pushes our button in a very positive way. And I find the wonderful thing about this Rule is that it invariably isn't the things that cost money that have this power. The things that lift us are usually magical in some way – a particular view or person, a pet or a child, a favourite book or film that we turn to, to help us recharge. It might be a state of mind that we arrive at through some ritual such as going to a place of worship or meditating. It might be a certain piece of music that lightens our heart. For some it will be reorganizing their stamp collection, for others it will be doing charity work or being a volunteer (there's nothing like doing something for others or for a greater good to take you out of yourself). Whatever it is, make sure you have it, know it and use it. No good having a piece of music that always lifts your mood if you don't play it occasionally.

I guess we all need something in our lives that takes us out of ourselves and, perhaps, stops us taking ourselves too seriously. Whether it's a dog, a child or a chat with a lonely person at a day centre, there needs to be something that makes you realize that all the stuff that's getting to you isn't that important and reminds you of the simple pleasures in life.

> ## NO GOOD HAVING A PIECE OF MUSIC THAT ALWAYS LIFTS YOUR MOOD IF YOU DON'T PLAY IT OCCASIONALLY

RULE 56

Only the good feel guilty

Bad people don't feel guilty, they are too busy being bad. Good people feel guilty *because* they are good and they feel they have done wrong, let somebody down, made a mistake or screwed up somewhere. Good people have a conscience. Bad people don't. If you do feel guilty, that's a good sign. It shows you are on the right track. But you have to know how to deal with it, because guilt is a terribly selfish emotion. It is wasteful and pointless.

> ## IF YOU DO FEEL GUILTY,
> ## THAT'S A GOOD SIGN

We have two choices: put it right or dump the guilt. Yes, we all make mistakes. We all screw up from time to time. We don't always do 'the right thing'. And if we've got a conscience, we will feel guilty sometimes. But guilt is utterly pointless unless it is acted on for the better. You would be better off feeling something else* if you aren't going to act on your guilt. If you hang around feeling guilty but don't do anything about it, then it's a waste of time and life.

---

* Self loathing, fear, panic – all good substitutes for guilt if you really must. But better just to let it go.

The first thing to do is to assess whether you really need to feel guilty. It could just be an overdeveloped conscience or sense of duty. If you are the kind of person always to volunteer, but just this once you say no, then there is no need to feel guilty. You'll know deep down if you've earned this one off. If you've a choice between doing something or not, then it's simple: do it or don't do it but without guilt. Make the choice with that in mind. Not doing it and feeling guilty is not an option.

If you *do* have cause to feel guilty, then if you can, put it right. That's the simplest course of action. And what if you can't put things right? Then learn the lesson, make a resolution, dump the guilt and move on. If it keeps on gnawing away at you, you have to find a way to put it behind you.

If you can't say anything nice, don't say anything at all

It is very easy to moan, to complain, to criticize. It is much harder to always find something nice to say about a situation or a person. But think of it now as a huge challenge. Saying something nice is hard because our natural inclination is to moan. If someone asks how the weekend camping went, it's easier to start on the bad weather and the problems with the campsite and the annoying behaviour of the people in the next-door caravan than it is about the joy of being with people you wanted to be with and in a fantastic setting. When a friend asks how you're getting on with your boss, the things they do that really annoy you usually spring to mind before the upsides.

No matter how horrid someone is, there is always something about them that is good. Your job is to find that good bit and highlight it, speak about it, draw attention to it. Same with a situation that seems troublesome. I remember reading once of someone who was on the Metro in Paris during a major strike. It was chaos and people were shoving and pushing and it was pretty horrendous. There was a woman with a small child there and it could have been quite scary. She bent down to the child and said quite brightly, 'This, my dear, is what they call an adventure'. It has become a pet phrase of mine in times of crisis and trouble.

When asked your opinion of someone, something, somewhere, you need to find something good to say, something flattering and positive. There is ample evidence that being positive has many benefits but the most noticeable is that people will gravitate towards you and not even know why. That positive air about you is attractive. People like being around those who are upbeat, positive, happy and confident. We need to bite our tongues more and say good things more often.

Obviously if you are only going to say good things, then this cuts out back-biting, gossiping, slagging off, telling tales, being rude about people, complaining (you are allowed to point out defects or problems but in a constructive way). And that could leave you with a big gap to fill.

Before opening your mouth, try – just for a week – to find something good to say. It's one of those things that will amaze you by how it improves your life, but don't take my word for it – just try it. And if all else fails, and you really can't think of anything positive to say at all, then don't say anything. At all.

> ## 'THIS, MY DEAR, IS WHAT THEY CALL AN ADVENTURE'

PARTNERSHIP
RULES

We all need to love and to be loved. Most of us want the comfort of a relationship and the closeness of companionship that such a relationship brings. We aren't islands and we do need to share together with someone very dear and close to us. 'Tis human nature. We wouldn't be the fantastic people we are without that need to give and to be given to.

But, and this is a big but, (does my but look big in this?) human relationships being what they are, this is an enormous area in which to make mistakes, fall flat on our faces and to generally make a dog's dinner out of the whole business. We need Rules here like they are going out of style. We need all the guidance we can get. Right, that's enough about me.

But, seriously, we do all need help and sometimes it pays to come at the subject from a slightly different angle. What follows are some unusual Rules to get you thinking about your relationship from a new perspective.

None of this is revolutionary, but these are the Rules I've noticed those who have successful, productive, sustaining, long-lasting and nurturing relationships have about them. They are also the ones having exciting, stimulating, extremely close and powerful relationships.

Accept the differences, embrace what you have in common

'Sugar and spice and all things nice . . . slugs and snails and puppy dogs' tails' – isn't that how the rhyme goes? So which are you? The slugs and snails or the sugar and spice? Chances are, you're a bit of both. Look, it's true that men and women have differences. We would be fools if we didn't accept and recognize that. But we're not so different that we are separate species – or from separate planets, as some would have us believe. We actually have more in common than we have differences. If we embrace those things we have in common and accept what is different, we might get on a whole lot better instead of treating each other as if we were separate species. A same-sex relationship avoids the assumption that you're inherently different, but you're still two very different people.

A relationship is, if you like, a team made up of initially two people (later the team may get swamped by lots of junior team members) who both bring talents and skills and resources to the relationship. Every team needs different people with different qualities to achieve things and to make the project work. If you are both strong leaders, quick decision makers and impulsive hotheads, then who is going to see to the detail and finish off projects? Who is going to do the work instead of just generating the ideas? Never mind just accepting the differences – see the benefits! Try to view differences in the light of them being special talents – differences that could be used effectively to make your team function better.

EVERY TEAM NEEDS DIFFERENT PEOPLE WITH DIFFERENT QUALITIES

And what of the things you have in common? It can be great (shared views, shared tastes) but it doesn't always make life simple (shared love of being right, shared need to be in control). If you are both genuine leaders, you might both be wrestling for the driver's seat. Instead, agree to take it in turn to lead. The things in common should be celebrated and used – in combination or alternately – to really fire you both up and make the relationship special and successful.

Look, you're in this together – whatever 'this' is – and you need to work together to make it successful. If you combine the talents you have in common, you will get a lot further and have an easier time of it than if you both pull in different directions. Strip away the layers and we are all human, all frightened, all vulnerable, all trying to make some sort of sense out of our lives. If we focus on the differences and make a big deal out of them, we risk losing the input and contribution of somebody who can help to lighten our load and make the journey more fun. All those crass internet jokes – if a woman was a computer she would be this, and if a man was a car he'd be that – really don't help. Real life isn't like that.

Allow* your partner the space to be themselves

It's a funny old thing but we often fall in love with someone because they are independent, forceful, powerful, in charge, in control and very much out in the world. Then, the second we've captured them, so to speak, we try to change them. We come over all jealous if they carry on being as independent; as if being in a relationship with us somehow limits them, ties them down, cuts their wings off.

Before we met them, they managed quite well without us. The second we meet them, we start giving them advice, restricting their choices, limiting their vision and dreams, curtailing their freedom. We need to stand back and give them the freedom to be themselves.

A lot of people say that the magic of their relationship has worn off, that there is no sparkle there any more and that they have grown apart. And then when you look into it a bit more deeply you find two people locked in a symbiotic relationship of mistrust, oppression and niggling encroachment. They don't give each other any space at all, let alone space to be themselves.

So what can we do? Firstly stand back and see your partner as they were when you first met them. What attracted you? What was special about them? What turned you on?

---

* Yes, yes I know I said 'Allow'. It is a joke, don't write in . . .

Now look at them. What is different? What has gone and what has been replaced? Are they still the same independent person or have you eroded their space, confidence, independence, vitality? Maybe not, that seems a bit harsh, but unconsciously we do tend to rein them in a bit and they do lose their sparkle.

> # WHAT ATTRACTED YOU?
> # WHAT WAS SPECIAL
> # ABOUT THEM? WHAT
> # TURNED YOU ON?

You have to encourage them to step outside the cosiness of the relationship and rediscover their energy and vitality. They may need to spend some time rediscovering their talents and skills at being independent. And you may need to sit on your hands at times to avoid reining them in again. So encourage, stand back, sit on your hands, push and be there. Tall order. Most successful relationships have an element, and a big one, of independence. Two people spend time apart to bring something back to the relationship with them. This is healthy. This is good. This is grown-up.

Be nice

It is very easy in the hurly-burly of modern life and the complex sparring of a day-to-day relationship to forget that we are dealing with a real live human being here and not just someone we bounce off as we go along. It is easy to start to take someone for granted, to think we've thanked them or praised them or said 'please', when instead we ignored them, were rude by the guilty sin of omission, disregarded them and generally behaved like they were pond life by default.

To make the relationship go with a zing, you have to go back to square one and start being courteous again in the old-fashioned sense of the word. You have to reintroduce yourselves to each other as respectful, tactful individuals who are going to start again being pleasant, kind, civil and polite. From now on you will say 'please' and 'thank you' no matter how many times a day it is necessary. Be thoughtful. Be complimentary. Give gifts without there being any reason for doing so. Ask questions to show you are interested in what your partner is saying.

> ## GO BACK TO SQUARE ONE AND START BEING COURTEOUS AGAIN

Be solicitous of their health, welfare, dreams, hopes, workload, interests and pleasure. Take time to help them. Take time to focus on their needs and wants. Take time to just be there for them – just to listen, show an interest, show that you still love them. Don't allow benign neglect to ruin your relationship.

We treat strangers exceedingly well and usually reserve our best attentions for people we work with. Our partner gets missed, lost in the bustle of it all. In fact we should treat them better than anyone else. After all, they are supposed to be the most important person in the world to us. It makes sense to show them this is true.

Of course, if you already do all this you must excuse me reminding you to.

I was reading about a chap who kept buying his wife new handbags – always unsuitable ones, not big enough or tough enough for her needs. She tried explaining that she was quite happy to buy her own bags as she was a grown-up, but he had got it into his head that his idea of 'style' was so much better than hers. In the end she bought him a bag and that shut him up for a bit. I thought this a wonderfully Zen solution. She didn't get cross or yell at him, but just gently poked fun at him. Brilliant.

You want to do what?

Just because we come together to be a couple for however long, doesn't mean we are joined at the hip and have to think the same, do the same, feel the same, react the same. I have noticed that the most successful relationships are the ones where the couple is strong together but also strong apart. The best relationships are the ones where both people are supportive of each other's interest even if they aren't their own.

Being supportive of your partner and what they want to do means you have to be very centred yourself not to feel jealous or mistrustful or resentful. You have to be prepared for them to be independent, strong, out in the world separate from you. It can be hard. It can ask a lot of you. It can be a real test of how much you care and how protective you tend to be.

The more freedom you give/allow/tolerate/encourage, the more likely they will be to reciprocate and return. If a partner feels they are encouraged and trusted, they are much less likely to 'stray' or want out because they feel hemmed in or caged. The more supportive you are, the more they will feel they are being treated kindly and that is a good thing.

But what if you disagree with what they want to do? Then you have to look at your own stuff I'm afraid. You see, they are a separate human being and entitled to do pretty well whatever they want to do – assuming it isn't hurtful to you or in any serious way jeopardizes the relationship (such as sleeping with other people or committing crimes) – and it is your role to be supportive. You may need to question what it is about what they want to do that you find hard to go along with. This might be more about you than them.

Ask yourself – if they do this, if they go ahead, what's the worst that can happen? They make a mess of your floor, ruin part of the garden, spend money on something you don't really want, aren't around much for a week. Now compare that to the thought of them leaving, or living with you frustrated and unhappy. Which is worse?

Of course, just because they say they want to do something doesn't mean they will. Some very stubborn types will, however, be more likely to go ahead and do it just because you're objecting to everything they mention. Say 'yes' and they might well never bother anyway.

If you look ahead to Rule 70, you will read about how you should treat your partner *better* than your best friend, and being supportive is part of this. We forget that our partner is a separate entity. We forget that they too have dreams and plans and unfulfilled ambitions. It is our job to encourage them to find their path, to realize those ambitions, to stretch themselves to their fullest extent, to be complete and satisfied and fulfilled. It is not our job to put them down, ridicule their dreams, belittle their plans or laugh at their ambitions. It is not our job to discourage them, put them off, place obstacles in their path or restrict them in any way. It is our job to encourage them to soar.

> # YOU HAVE TO BE PREPARED FOR THEM TO BE INDEPENDENT, STRONG, OUT IN THE WORLD SEPARATE FROM YOU

Be the first to say sorry

Don't care who started it. Don't care what it was about. Don't care who is right and who is wrong. Don't care whose game it was. You are both behaving like spoilt brats and should go to your room at once. No seriously, we all fall out from time to time, that's human nature. From now on, if you want to be a committed Rules Player, and I can see from the glint in your eye you do, you will be the first to say sorry. That's it. End of Rule. Why? Because that's what Rules Players do. We are the first. We take great pride in being first because we are so firm in our own sense of ourselves that we don't feel any loss of pride if we say sorry. We don't feel threatened or challenged or weak. We can say sorry and still be strong. We can say sorry *and* retain our dignity and respect.

We will say sorry because we *are* sorry. We are sorry to have become embroiled in an argument of any sort and have by the very nature of arguing forgotten at least five Rules.

> ## WE CAN SAY SORRY *AND*
> ## RETAIN OUR DIGNITY
> ## AND RESPECT

You see, if it has got as far as a falling out, no matter how trivial or minor, we have already committed a few cardinal mistakes and thus should be the first to say sorry because we are in the wrong, no matter what the argument is about. Arguing is what we are saying sorry for. Never mind what it was about, we are saying sorry first because we are noble, kind, generous in spirit, dignified, mature, sensible and good. I know, I know, gosh we have to be all these things and still say sorry. Tough call, tall order. Just do it and see how good it makes you feel. The view is always fantastic from the moral high ground.

And what if you are both reading this book? Heavens. Then you must not tell each other you are – Rule 1 – but then race to be the first to say sorry. Could be interesting. Let me know how you get on.

Saying sorry has many benefits, even if it does stick in your throat a little. Not only does it give you the moral advantage, but it also defuses tension, gets rid of bad feelings and clears the air. Chances are that if you say sorry first, your partner will also probably be humbled into apologizing. Maybe.

Always remember you are not apologizing for the sin or crime or faux pas you have committed – you are apologizing for being so immature to have argued in the first place, apologizing for losing your rag, apologizing for forgetting Rules, apologizing for being boorish or argumentative or stubborn or rude or childish or whatever. You can come out of your room now.

Go that extra step in trying to please them

What? You have to be the first to say you are sorry, encourage and support them, give them freedom, be supportive, be nice, and now I am saying go that extra step in trying to please them as well. Strewth, anyone would think you were doing this out of love. You'd think this was for someone you adored and worshipped and respected and had great affection for – someone you really cared about. Precisely. That is exactly what it's about. This is about going an extra step to please the person who means the most to you in all the world, the person you love and cherish and care about, the person who is the most important human being in your life. This is about your love, your companion, your treasure, your soul mate, your lover and friend. So what's your problem? Why wouldn't you want to do this? Why wouldn't you be doing it already?

So if we want to, what is it we are supposed to be doing? Easy, thinking ahead. Planning birthdays that are more than just a present, a card, some flowers and a couple of drinks down the pub – and that's if they're lucky this year. It's thinking about what they would like, what they might want, for birthdays, special treats, days off, long weekends and anniversaries. It's thinking of extravagances, luxuries, indulgences. It's going out of your way to find out what they would really, really like and then giving it to them. And I'm not talking money here. This is about surprising them, finding little things to delight them and show that you have thought of them. Arranging things in advance to let them know how special they are and how much you care and how important they are.

This is finding ways to delight them beyond the normal, way beyond what is expected, further than anyone else would. This is a fantastic opportunity to be creative, adventurous, wacky, unusual, caring and loving all at the same time. Haven't got the time? Then you must check your priority list. What could be more important than delighting your lover and partner and friend? (Yes, it is the same person, not three people.)

> # WHY WOULDN'T YOU WANT TO DO THIS? WHY WOULDN'T YOU BE DOING IT ALREADY?

Know when to listen and when to act

I don't know if it's harder for us chaps to learn this one but I find it tough. Whenever anyone has a problem, I want to rush off and do something. Doesn't really matter what, just so long as I am doing something, anything.

In actual fact what is often required of me is that I sit down and listen. I am not being told troubles and problems just so I can be all macho and rescue someone or leap to their defence or single-handedly take on the world for them (in fact be a hero). What is needed is a sympathetic ear, a shoulder perhaps to cry on, an 'Oh, that must be awful for you' sort of response, a counsellor's approach and a full and rapt attention with eye contact. That's the tricky bit. As soon as I've heard the problem I've switched off, or rather I've switched to working out what the solution must be.

But for me, when I have a problem I don't want to hear sympathetic noises and encouraging sounds. I don't want a heart space where I can share. I just want a solution, an offer of help, an extra pair of hands, a stout length of rope and a screwdriver.*

But then all my problems are object related and need practical solutions – a chap's sort of thing. All the problems that I find the hardest to just listen to are person related and need a completely different approach. Knowing when to listen and when to act is an extremely useful skill to develop. I still constantly need to stop myself interrupting someone who is sharing a problem with me by saying, 'Hold it right there, I can see exactly what this needs' and then rushing off to fetch my tool kit.

---

* Or whatever it takes to fix my particular problem.

Of course, some problems don't actually have solutions, that's not why we're being told them. We are being told so we can be part of the process, and that may be sympathy, grief, shock, empathy, kindness, emotional advice, hand holding. Knowing when to offer tea and sympathy or a tool kit and a stout rope instead is the skill to learn and a good Rules Player gets it right. (Yes, yes, I know, I still get it wrong far too often.)

> # KNOWING WHEN TO OFFER TEA AND SYMPATHY OR A TOOL KIT IS THE SKILL TO LEARN

Have a passion for your life together

So you two met and fell in love and resolved to spend your lives together. And you are, I hope. But at what level? I'm not being funny here but serious (for once). Just sort of living together, going through the days, not really connecting isn't good enough, I'm afraid. You have to have a passion for your life together. A what? A passion. Being together has to be a strong bond, a common sharing of experience, a dream-fulfilling romance that carries you both along. Love isn't for the half dead, the sound asleep (or even the merely dozing off), the can't be bothered to make the effort any more. You have to make the effort. You have to stay awake, in touch, in tune. You have to share dreams and goals and ambitions and plans. You have to have passion for being with each other.

Look, I know that all relationships go through peaks and troughs. I know we get complacent and even a little bored at times. But you are dedicating your life to someone else's happiness in a way, and that requires focus, strength, passion, drive, enthusiasm and effort. What's that? You're not dedicating yourself to someone else's happiness? Then what are you doing? That's what a relationship is all about in a sense. And if you're not doing that, what do you think you are doing?

You have to really care, to still be in love, to want your partner to be fulfilled, successful, happy, complete.

In an ideal world you only get one crack of the whip at this. (I know that lots of people have several partners over a lifetime but I assume the aim is always to stay together for life and not to split up.) This is your chance to have a really good strong relationship based on mutual trust, responsibility, shared happiness, drive and the pursuit of excellence. It isn't? What is it then? It has to be if you are going to get the maximum out of it. Your partner isn't just there for someone to chat to when you get a bit fed up and want some company. They are there because they love you and you them. They are there for you both to have a relationship. If that isn't as much as anyone needs as an incentive to live life to the full and have a passion, then I don't know what is.

> # YOU ARE DEDICATING YOUR LIFE TO SOMEONE ELSE'S HAPPINESS

Make sure your love making is making love

So! We get to talk about sex now? Well, actually no. What I'm going to talk about is love. If you are in love and being loved, it is part of the natural process to make love and this is both fun and fraught with all sorts of problems. In a relationship, as successful Rules Players, we have to be kind, courteous, reverential, stimulating, creative, respectful, thoughtful, considerate and sexual. Within that sexual relationship we have to be all those things as well – respectful, kind etc. We have to take our partner's needs and wants into consideration without subjecting ourselves to anything we wouldn't want to do or find embarrassing or difficult. We have the right to privacy. We have the right to respect. We have the right to be held in high esteem.

And so does our partner. Consideration has to be the key word. We have to be considerate of what they need, like, want, are capable of doing. We have to be courteous.

> **WE HAVE THE RIGHT TO PRIVACY, TO RESPECT, TO BE HELD IN HIGH ESTEEM**

And yes, within all this there is a space and a place for passion, for excitement, for rude, raunchy sex. We don't have to be tame to be considerate, we don't have to be inhibited to be kind, we don't have to be tame just because we are being respectful. This isn't about being unexciting or dreary or boring just because we are taking our partner's safety, privacy, health, intimacy into account. Even the most passionate lovers can be kind to each other while tearing each other's clothes off and having very physical sex – the two can go together.

Having sex with someone you love – making love if you like – is an honour in a way. (For me, just having someone these days who is prepared to take their clothes off at the same time as I do is an honour . . .) Making love is as close as we are ever going to get to another human being, as intimate as it is ever going to be. If we don't move respectfully in this arena, then what are we doing? And respect grows out of knowledge – knowledge of not only what our partner likes best but of the whole process. We should be as skilful as possible and, if we aren't, it is something we can spend a bit of time learning about. There is no shame in learning. We can't all be born the best drivers *and* the best lovers in the world.

Keep talking

Yep, gotta keep talking. When there is trouble afoot it's talking that will get us out of it. When we are going through bad patches, it is talking it out that will see us through. When we are optimistic and excited, it is talking that will help our partner share it.

If we aren't talking there is something wrong. If we aren't talking, what are we doing? Talking helps us understand, listen, share, communicate.

Lots of people assume that silence means there's a problem, something wrong. Of course, we don't need to fill all the silences but there are some pretty basic rules of etiquette when it comes to talking to each other:

- Acknowledge that your partner has spoken to you – and no, a grunt or a sigh isn't what I mean.

- Make some recognition every few seconds that you are still awake, alive, in the room, interested, paying attention – this may be a nod, a yes or no, a noise of encouragement (hmm, oh).

- Be aware that talking is part of your duties as a lover/partner and you should be good at it.

- Good talking leads to good sex – if you aren't talking you aren't flirting, holding hands, seducing. By talking we are committing the act known as foreplay.

- Talking helps resolve problems, silence only amplifies them.

- Talking keeps you together – it's what you used to do when you first fell in love, remember?

There is obviously a time and a place for silences (see Rule 64) – but talking is healthy, productive, companionable, friendly, loving, kind and fun. Silences can be boring, unhelpful, destructive and threatening. Obviously there is quality talking and there is rabbiting on. Make sure you don't just chatter away to fill the silences with meaningless trivia. Talking has to have some purpose although nattering is fine. Just wittering isn't. So talk sensibly now.

> IF WE AREN'T TALKING
> THERE IS SOMETHING
> WRONG. IF WE AREN'T
> TALKING, WHAT ARE
> WE DOING?

Respect privacy

'I want to be alone . . .' Each and every one of us has a God-given right to respect, privacy, trust, honesty. But of all of them, it is privacy that is the most sacrosanct, inviolate, untouchable.

You must respect your partner's privacy as they must yours. If you don't, you have to question all those other things – trust, respect, honesty – as well. If they are all missing, what you've got there isn't a relationship and quite frankly I don't know *what* it is, except that it belongs in the morgue. So we'll assume you have a good and healthy relationship. This means you have respect for your partner's privacy. In all areas.

If they choose not to discuss something with you, then that is their right and you do not have the right to:

- wheedle

- threaten

- emotionally blackmail

- bribe

- withhold privileges

- try and find out by underhand means and methods.

And no, charming them out of it counts as a no-no as well. Privacy isn't just about not opening someone's post or listening to their telephone messages or reading their emails when they're not looking. Privacy is also about making sure they can carry out their ablutions on their own – we all need a certain degree of grace and dignity in our lives and separate bathroom activities is the standard bottom line actually. Sharing a bathroom all the time isn't desirable, at least not for all activities. Ugh, how horrid. If you can't have separate bathrooms at least have some separate privacy in the bathroom. I know shared baths and the like can be very intimate and romantic, but you don't have to cut your toenails or squeeze your blackheads in front of each other. Don't do it. Winston Churchill said the reason he managed to stay married for 56 years – or however long it was – was separate bathrooms. So keep yourself to yourself in your more intimate ablutions and make sure you don't intrude on anyone else's privacy. You can extend this Rule to everyone else in the entire universe, not just your partner.

If you feel a need to intrude on someone else's privacy, you have to take a long hard look at yourself and fathom out why. The truth may be unpalatable, but you have to know it.

> **IF YOU FEEL A NEED TO INTRUDE ON SOMEONE ELSE'S PRIVACY, YOU HAVE TO TAKE A LONG HARD LOOK AT YOURSELF AND FATHOM OUT WHY**

Check you both have the same shared goals

When we first meet and fall in love, we think we know pretty well everything we can about our love. We have so much in common. It all seems so easy, so intuitive, so natural. Of course we want the same. Of course we are two sides of the same coin. Of course we are going to share life's highway together.

Wrong, wrong, wrong. The highway will diverge at times and if you aren't on the ball you will lose sight of each other completely and forever. You have to keep checking that you are both singing from the same map so to speak, both heading for the same destination, both going in the same direction even.

So what are your shared goals? Where do you both think you're going? No, don't guess here. Don't make them assumed goals or even guessed goals. You have to *know* what your partner thinks are the shared goals – and what you think. They might be a world apart. Or then again they might be very close. You'll only know if you ask – discreetly of course, don't want to frighten the horses here.

And you have to differentiate between shared goals and shared dreams. We all have dreams – the cottage by the sea, the trip round the world, the Ferrari, the second home in Malibu, the purpose-built wine cellar (fully stocked of course), the Olympic-size swimming pool – but goals are different. Goals are to have children (or not); to travel a lot; to retire early and live in Spain; to bring up the children to be happy, well-adjusted people; to stay together (!); to move to the countryside/town; to downsize together and work from home; to run your own business together; to get a dog. I guess dreams are things you aim to get one day and goals are what you are doing together. Dreams are acquisitions that either of you could want and goals are shared aims that you need each other for because without the other the goal is pretty meaningless.

This Rule is about reviewing. To review, you have to talk to your partner about where it is you both think you're going and what you're doing. It doesn't have to be heavy. This can be a light review just to touch base and check that you are both on the same track. It doesn't have to be too detailed, just simple questions to confirm a general similar direction, rather than trying to map out an A-to-Z of your future life together.

> **YOU HAVE TO TALK TO YOUR PARTNER ABOUT WHERE IT IS YOU BOTH THINK YOU'RE GOING**

Treat your partner better than your best friend

I was talking to a friend about this Rule the other day and she disagreed with me emphatically. She said you had to treat your friends better because you knew them better and you owed them more loyalty. I then went on to talk to another friend and she said that wasn't the case. You treated your partner better because you knew them less well. Intriguing. My point is you should treat your partner better than your friends because your partner is both lover *and* friend. And ideally *best* friend.

If they're not, then who is? And why? Is it because they are the opposite sex and you need a same-sex best friend? Or are they the same sex and you need an opposite-sex best friend? Is it because you don't see a lover as a friend? (If you do answer yes to this, what *do* you see your partner as . . . what is their role or function in being your partner?)

Again, all this is about being conscious. Treating your partner better than your best friend means you have given this some thought and made a conscious decision to do so – or not if it's the case.

I would have thought treating your partner better than your best friend would have been a given. This means not interfering, respecting their privacy, treating them like independent grown-ups. You only have to look around to see couples who treat each other like small children, nagging, scolding, arguing, criticizing, nit-picking. They wouldn't do it with their friends, so why do they do it with the one person who is supposed to mean heaven and earth to them?

WHAT *DO* YOU SEE YOUR PARTNER AS . . . WHAT IS THEIR ROLE OR FUNCTION IN BEING YOUR PARTNER?

I'll give you an example. You are a passenger in a car being driven by a friend. They make a foolish error (though not a dangerous one). You would probably start teasing and laugh a lot. Now imagine the same scenario but with your partner who has messed up. Do you:

- make them feel very small?

- not let them forget it in a long while?

- tell everyone else?

- take over the driving for a while on the grounds they're not to be trusted?

- treat them the same as you would a friend and laugh a lot?

Hopefully the last one, but watch other couples in similar situations and see what they do.

Contentment is a high aim

If you ask a lot of people what they want in life, they say, 'Oh, just to be happy I guess'. Same goes if you ask what they want for their children, 'I don't mind what they do as long as they are happy'. You'd be better off wishing that you or your children could be astronauts or brain surgeons – at least you're in with a sporting chance then. You can train. They can qualify.

Happiness is such an illusory thing that spending too much time chasing it is not very worthwhile. Happiness is one end of a spectrum – misery being the other end. It is a state of extreme, just as misery represents the other end. If you check back at the times in your life when you've been happy – or thought you might have been – I'll bet there were other extreme feelings involved. The birth of a child? Excitement yes. Wonder yes. Relief at a successful birth. Yes. But happiness? I'm not sure.

People think they'll be happy on holiday when they mean relaxed or stimulated or freed from their cares – and indeed they are. Aiming for happiness is one of those 'bigger is best' things. You're never going to make it because there is no top-end limit. You just have to go on aiming for even bigger all the time. Instead of aiming for happy, it's better to aim for contentment. Now that's attainable. That's a worthy goal.

This applies especially to relationships – both to the quest to find Mr or Mrs Right and in what happens when you do. Most of us want to fall madly head-over-heels in love. Big chemistry – fireworks, butterflies, unbelievable feelings. It's brilliant. It's extreme. But that intensity can't and won't last. You have to go back to reality sometime. You have to get on with your life. No one can live at that intensity, that lofty altitude all the time. Contentment is what you hope for after the elation has worn off and you settle back into a relaxed and happy simplicity. In fact, contentment is the worthier aim, because it lasts.

And so if you find you are with somebody where there is no big firework display, palpitations and extreme feelings but there is a baseline contentment and warmth and love – be happy with that.

> # CONTENTMENT IS WHAT YOU HOPE FOR AFTER THE ELATION HAS WORN OFF

You don't both have to have the same rules

Lots of couples make the assumption that everything has to be the same for both of them – that you have to have the same set of rules for both partners. Not true. You can operate under different rules for important areas. The happiest relationships, the most successful, the strongest, are where both parties see the need for flexibility in their rules and adjust their relationship accordingly.

I expect you want an example? Of course you do. Let's suppose one of you is fanatically tidy and the other fanatically messy (whatever that is). Normally you would have one going on at the other all the time about how messy/tidy the other is. There would be rows and problems. That's because you are both trying to work to the same rule – we both have to be tidy/ we both have to be messy. How about a different rule? I can be messy; you can be tidy. I can have areas where I can be messy and you have areas where you can be tidy. Now we don't row because we have a different rule. I don't have to be tidy when it isn't in my nature and you don't have to be messy when it isn't in your nature.

Another example? My wife hates being teased and she hates being tickled. Me? I'm not bothered. She has the rule that she is not to be tickled – or teased – and my rule is I can.* You may be the kind of person who wants to know where your partner is, whereas they're not bothered about where you are and doesn't expect you to report on it. You can then have a rule where your partner tells you where they're going, to reassure you, but you

---

* No, this is only for my wife. Of course you can't come round and tickle or tease me.

don't need to keep them completely in the picture as they are not worried.

Your partner may need constant reassurance that you love them and may need to be told several times a day. You might prefer to be told less frequently but when it's genuinely felt – so you would have a rule that you'd mention it often but they didn't have to say it back every time. Different strokes for different folks.

> # THE HAPPIEST RELATIONSHIPS ARE WHERE BOTH PARTIES SEE THE NEED FOR FLEXIBILITY IN THEIR RULES

FAMILY AND FRIENDS RULES

If you imagine yourself as the centre of your own universe, then you are the very hub. The next circle around you is your lover, your partner; this is your closest, most intimate relationship. The next circle to that is your family and friends. These are the people you love the most, choose to spend most time with, love you the most. These are the people you can relax with, kick off your shoes and be yourself. But there are still Rules. There is still a right way to treat them and a not-so-right way. You still have to behave with honour, dignity, respect. You have responsibilities towards both your children and your parents. You have a duty to your siblings. You have obligations, which have to be taken seriously, to your friends.

You have a whole raft of hats to wear – parent, friend, child, brother/sister, uncle/aunt, godparent, niece/nephew, cousin – and a whole set of Rules and duties to perform. The next section is guidance on how best to wear all these hats.

As we go through this life we have to interact with other people. We rub up against them (emotionally) all the time and we have to have Rules to govern our behaviour so we do right by them, to steer us through tricky situations, new experiences and ongoing close relationships.

If we want our relationships with our family and friends to be successful and for them to think the very best of us, then we do need to give those relationships some thought – a conscious approach rather than sailing on asleep at the wheel like most people. By consciously being aware of what we are doing we can improve those relationships, iron out the problems, encourage others and generally spread a bit of warmth and happiness as we go. What could be finer?

RULE 73

If you are going to be a friend, be a good friend

Being a real friend is a tremendous responsibility. You have to be loyal, honest (but not too honest), sincere, reliable, dependable, friendly (stands to reason really), pleasant, open, sociable (not much point having friends if you're not going to be sociable is there?), responsive, welcoming and gracious. You also have to be forgiving at times, be prepared to offer help, support and sympathy. At the same time you don't want to be taken advantage of or have the wool pulled over your eyes. And you may have to be brutally candid at times and be prepared to risk the friendship by being so. Yet equally there are times you need to hold your tongue and keep your opinion to yourself. They are your friends, not clones of you – they do things differently. You have to be counsellor, confessor, priest, helper, companion, friend, confidant(e) and comrade. You have to offer the friendship enthusiasm, dedication, determination, creativity, interest, passion and drive.

And this is all what *you* have to do. What do they have to do? Well, in an ideal world the same. If they fail to do any of this, you will still carry on being their friend, being forgiving, being supportive and being there.

And I guess if you have to take anything away from this Rule, the most important bit is being there. You are there when they are going through it and not just there for the good times. You will be there when they need you in the early hours, the dark days, the times of trouble and stress. You will be there to hold their hand, let them cry on your shoulder, lend them a hanky, pat them on the back and make them endless cups of tea. And you will tell them to cheer up, not to worry, stop being such a fool, whatever it takes to get them up and at it again.

> # THE MOST IMPORTANT
> # BIT IS BEING THERE
> # . . . AND NOT JUST
> # FOR THE GOOD TIMES

You will be there to give them good advice. You will be there just to listen at times. You will be there when you don't want to be. You will be there when all their other friends have fallen by the wayside. You will be there no matter what.

Someone once said that a real friend is someone you can be having a conversation with as they get on a plane, you don't see them for ten years and when they arrive back they carry on the conversation as they get off the plane like a moment hadn't passed. That's exactly how it is between good friends.

Never be too busy for loved ones

It is very easy in the rush of living to overlook people close to us. I do it. I have brothers who are very special, very close to me and I forget to phone, forget to stay in touch. Not because I don't care but because I am too busy. Unforgivable. Every now and then I'll complain that I haven't heard from them. But of course it is me not staying in touch just as much as it is them. We have to make time, because if we don't, time slips past so fast that a few weeks become months, and then years are added on before we know it.

It's the same with children. Parents all harbour a secret fantasy of, 'Wouldn't it be nice to return to the Victorian ideal of seeing them for an hour before bedtime when nanny has them all bathed and pyjama-ed and ready with the muffins and jam?' sort of thing. Well, I know I do even if you don't. But the more time we put into our relationships – with children, siblings, parents, friends – the more we get out of them. It has to be us to make the move, to phone, to stay in touch. And what if they don't also do this? Fine. You're now the Rules Player.

This is what you do. You become incredibly successful at handling your life, at processing guilt (you don't have any because you phoned, you wrote, you stayed in touch), at forgiveness (they didn't phone or write or stay in touch), at relationships in general. You take the moral high ground and be the first to offer the hand of friendship, be the first to forgive and forget (and I don't care how serious the squabble was, Rules Players don't carry grudges, ever . . .).

No matter how busy your life is – and I hope these Rules will eliminate some stress and free up some time – you have to make time. You have to make quality time (sorry, I hate that expression as well) for all those around you to whom you make a difference. Those that love you get repaid in time – it's a fair exchange. They love you and you give them something of yourself, something precious. Yep, your time and attention. And you do this willingly, not as a chore. You do this with dedication and commitment and wholehearted enthusiasm – or you don't do it at all. There is no point spending quality time with your kids, for example, and using that time to catch up on work or read the paper or get tomorrow's lunchboxes ready. You have to be there entirely for them or they'll know your attention is elsewhere and they'll feel cheated.

So when the phone rings and it's your mum, grandmother or your old friend but you're really busy doing something, don't keep them on the phone making 'uh huh' noises while you simultaneously finish searching the web or writing that email. Either put everything down and give them your full attention, or ask if you can call them back later – and make sure you do. One day they might not be there – and then you will so desperately wish you'd actually listened. But then it'll be too late. So make time for the people who matter – today.

> # THE MORE WE PUT INTO OUR RELATIONSHIPS, THE MORE WE GET OUT OF THEM

RULE 75

Let your kids mess up for themselves – they don't need any help from you

I have children and I naturally want them to be happy and well adjusted and successful. But do I also harbour secret plans for them? Do I want them to be doctors? Lawyers? Diplomats? Scientists? Archaeologists? Palaeontologists? Writers? Entrepreneurs? The Pope (look, someone has to be the Pope and it may be some parent's ambition somewhere to see their child as the Pope)? Astronauts?

No. I don't think so. Hand on my heart, I can say I haven't ever had such ambitions for them. I do hope they're not listening but I can say that I've been disappointed on the odd occasion when their career choice has seemed a bit unusual – not their sort of thing at all. But you have to let them make mistakes. You can't steer them right all the time or they'd never learn for themselves.

And this is what this Rule is all about – giving your kids the space to mess things up. We've all done it. I was given immense freedom to screw up and I did it big time, magnificently, spectacularly. Result? I learned pretty quickly what worked and what didn't. I have a cousin who wasn't given anything like the same freedom and was much more protected and he didn't screw up anywhere nearly so badly. But later in life, and he'd be the first to agree with this, he managed his life in such an unfortunate way that his screw-up really was spectacular. We all have to make mistakes. Better to make them while we're young and have the resilience to bounce back.

Being a parent is about 75 per cent making it up as you go along. You too have the freedom to make mistakes. Trouble is that if you get it wrong as a parent, your mistakes can really affect someone's life adversely. That's why it can be really hard to stand back and watch our children make bad choices. We want to run to them and protect them, nurture them a bit more and keep them from harm. But they have to learn by getting it wrong. If we think they'll only learn by us telling them, then we are making a big mistake. They have to do life for themselves to really get to grips with it. It's real and they can't learn it from a book or from us or from the television. They can only learn it by getting their fingers burnt. Your job is to stand by with the elastoplast and the antiseptic and a kiss to make it better.

You are of course allowed to ask leading questions: Are you sure that's a good idea? Have you thought this one through? And what happens after you've done that? Can you afford to take that much time off? Won't it hurt a bit? Didn't you try something like this before? You can also do this with friends when you can see they are about to make a big mistake but you don't want to be the killjoy. Try not to make your questions sound too judgemental or moany or they'll ignore you and go ahead just to be stubborn.

> ## YOU CAN'T STEER THEM RIGHT ALL THE TIME OR THEY'D NEVER LEARN FOR THEMSELVES

RULE 76

Have a little respect and forgiveness for your parents

This one may or may not affect you. Personally, as I am now technically an orphan, it shouldn't affect me. But it does. Big time. I was brought up with two major dysfunctional features. A missing father and a difficult mother. I have siblings with the same background. We have all handled it differently. I found it easier to come to terms with my mother once I too had children and could see what a difficult job it is. I could then also see that some people are intuitively, naturally good at it. And some people are, to be brutally frank, utterly useless at it. My mother fell into the latter category. Was that her fault? No. Should I blame her? No. Can I forgive her? There is nothing to forgive. She embarked on a life path for which she was ill-equipped, received no help, was lacking in any skill, and found extremely limiting and difficult. Result? She treated her children appallingly and we probably all need therapy. Or forgiveness and respect. Why should she be blamed for doing a difficult job badly? Hey, there are lots of areas in all our lives where we aren't very efficient or skilled or even enthusiastic.

Your parents do the best they can. And that might not be good enough for you but it is still the best they could do. They can't be blamed if they weren't very good at it. We can't all be fabulous parents.

And the absent father? That's OK too. We all make choices that others can judge as bad or unforgivable or just plain selfish and wrong. But we aren't there. We don't know what weaknesses people have or what drives them. Or indeed what is even going through their heads. We can't judge until we too have to make the same choice. And even then if we choose a different way, then that's fine, but we still can't judge or blame.

So, for the fact they brought you into the world, have a little respect and forgiveness. If they did a good job, then tell them. If you love them (and there is nothing that says you have to), then tell them. And if they were appalling at parenting, then forgive them and move on.

As offspring you do have a duty to be respectful. You have a responsibility to treat them kindly and be more than they are by being forgiving and non-judgemental. You *can* rise above your upbringing.

> THERE ARE LOTS OF AREAS
> IN ALL OUR LIVES WHERE
> WE AREN'T VERY EFFICIENT
> OR SKILLED OR EVEN
> ENTHUSIASTIC

Give your kids a break

We'll talk in a bit about what good parenting is – what your role as a parent is. First, let's look at this Rule – give your kids a break means to support and encourage your children. In fact this should be to support and encourage *all* children, not just your own. Children get a pretty poor deal of it. They get it in the neck from all directions and the word that figures most in their lives is 'no'. No, you can't do this. No, you're not old enough for this. No, you can't have that. No, you're not going there. No, you can't see that film.

Cast your mind back and see if it wasn't the same for you.

'No' is terribly easy for us to say. It's the word that trips so readily off the tongue. But to give support and encouragement we do have to train ourselves out of it. We have to learn to say 'yes'. Obviously we need to qualify our 'yes', depending on the age or skills or development of the child. But a resounding 'yes' gives them a great boost even if it is followed by a 'but not at the moment', or 'when you are old enough' or 'when you have saved up'.

> **THEY GET IT IN THE NECK FROM ALL DIRECTIONS AND THE WORD THAT FIGURES MOST IN THEIR LIVES IS 'NO'**

It is also easy to say to a child, 'You're not very good at that', or 'I wouldn't do that if I were you, you'll only fail'. Better to encourage them and let them learn that they might fail than to set the idea running in their mind beforehand. I know we all want to protect them from harm, from failure, from disappointment. But sometimes we have to push them forwards and shelve those worries for the moment.

Truly successful parents are the ones saying, 'Go on, you can do that, you'll be great at that, you'll be terrific'. By voicing such positive enforcement, our children get to believe in themselves and can do more, be more, achieve more. If we just say no they'll grow up with low self-esteem and lacking in confidence.

A friend recalls how she desperately wanted to be a ballet dancer when she was 6 years old. She was already showing the signs of being destined for her current 6 ft tall, large feet, athletic build – as far from a ballet dancer as you can imagine. Her parents must have been able to see this, and could have told her that really she should do something else. Like all-in wrestling for kids. But instead, they found her a ballet class. It didn't take long for her to realize that ballet wasn't right for her and she stopped going because it made her legs hurt. However, it was her choice to stop. And she left with her self-esteem intact. (She only wishes they hadn't taken the photos.)

Whatever they want to do, it is not your job to edit their dream, stand in their way, voice your concerns, limit their hopes or discourage them in any way. Your job is to give guidance while supporting and encouraging. Your job is to give them the resources to achieve whatever it is they want to. Whether they do or don't achieve is by the by. If they had the chance, that's everything.

Never lend money unless you are prepared to write it off

The full title of this Rule should actually be: Never lend money – to a friend or your children or siblings or even parents – unless you are prepared to write off either the money or the relationship.

There is a lovely story told, I think, about Oscar Wilde (correct me if I've got the wrong person) who borrowed a book from a friend and forgot to return it. His friend turned up and demanded the book back, by which time young Oscar had lost it. His friend asked Oscar if he wasn't jeopardizing the friendship by not returning the book. Oscar Wilde merely replied, 'Yes. But aren't you also doing the same thing by demanding it back?'

If you lend money – or a book or anything else – don't do it unless you are prepared for it to be lost, forgotten, not returned, broken, ignored, whatever.

If you are precious about it, then don't lend it in the first place. If it means a lot to you, keep it safe. If you do lend anything, including money, then don't expect to get it back if you value the friendship – or relationship. If you do get it back then that is a bonus. If you don't, well you were prepared for that in the first place.

Lots of parents make the mistake of lending money to their children and then getting all hurt and disappointed when they don't get repaid. But they have spent the child's entire life giving them money and then as soon as they get a bit grown up and go away to university or whatever, the parents suddenly start saying it's a loan and demand repayment. Of course the child isn't going to repay it. They haven't been trained to. It is unrealistic to expect them to do so. If they do, count your blessings and be grateful for the bonus.

Same with friends. Don't lend them anything if the non-return is going to matter to you. It is your choice after all. You don't have to lend anything to anyone. If you choose to do so, be prepared to write it off or don't do it. Obviously if the money means more to you than the friendship, then of course demand to be repaid – and add interest as well.

And the same goes for siblings or parents (goodness, don't ever lend money to them, they'll never pay it back). So who should you lend money to? Strangers of course. And they won't pay it back either.

IF YOU ARE PRECIOUS ABOUT IT, THEN DON'T LEND IT IN THE FIRST PLACE

Keep schtum

I have a friend who has three small children. She told me recently that before she had children she didn't really get the things that people with children told her. She wasn't always convinced by their claims of tiredness or logistical problems, she didn't necessarily believe that children could squabble that much or be such hard work, she sometimes just didn't understand what they were talking about. Even when she had two children, she didn't really get what people with more than two children were telling her. Now, however, she says she finally really gets it, and it just isn't like she'd imagined.

You'd have thought that if you had two children you'd know what life was like for people with three kids. But you don't. In fact, you don't even know what life is like for other people with two children who are different sexes from yours, or further apart in age, or when there's less money, or the parents are working different hours from you. Even apparently similar circumstances can be deceptively different.

And we all have our own personalities and values and strengths and weaknesses. I know one person who is widowed and hates spending time with happy couples because it reminds her what she's lost. I have another widowed friend who has no problem spending time with couples because she doesn't see it in relation to her own marriage. Neither is right or wrong, but both have their own histories and attitudes.

So what am I saying? Essentially, don't judge. Try walking a mile in someone else's moccasins before you presume to know what their life is like. My own mother had one of her children adopted when he was a few weeks old. For years I thought this was a terrible thing to do. But once I had children of my own, I realized that I had no way of assessing whether what she did was OK. She already had five children, she had been widowed and therefore the sole earner (in the 1950s, when that was even harder than it is now), and she was working all hours with no money for childcare. Would I have coped any better in her circumstances? I can't know.

This isn't easy. I'm just saying that we should think twice before we form an opinion. I'm also saying that since we can't judge anyone else's situation, we should keep quiet about their choices in life. It's not for us to tell even our nearest and dearest how we think they should act. For many of us, and I'm certainly including myself here, this can be one of the hardest Rules of all.

Think about how you feel when people try to tell you what to do. If you know what's right for you, you don't appreciate other people telling you what they think. They don't understand. No, not even your closest family really understand what it's like to be you. Even if you're making a mistake, you still want to be allowed to make it for yourself and to learn from it. And that's how we need to treat everyone else around us. Tough, ain't it? But necessary.

> **THINK ABOUT HOW YOU FEEL WHEN PEOPLE TRY TO TELL YOU WHAT TO DO**

There are no bad children

A certain phrase once crept out of Southern California and made its way to the UK. It made my blood boil: 'They're a good child who's done a bad thing.'

How it made me cringe. I hated it. I railed against it. This was the most awful bit of New Age PC-speak I had ever heard. But now I have to apologize. I have taken this one on board and, while I may never actually say 'They're a good child who's done a bad thing', I do endorse the sentiment. You see, there are no bad children. Yes, there may be children who do bad things. There may be children who do appalling things. But they are not bad. No matter how naughty my children are, they are not bad. They may make me climb the walls with their behaviour at times but when they have gone to sleep and you peep in at them, they are angelic little cherubs, utterly good, utterly perfect. Yes, what they do during the day, to get my dander up, may be naughty, may be bad behaviour, but they remain intrinsically good.

The only reason the behaviour is bad is because they are exploring the world and learning where the boundaries are. They have to make mistakes in order to find out what's what. It is only natural and quite normal.

The same goes for any other behaviour that is out of the ordinary. There are no clumsy children, only clumsy behaviour. There are no stupid children, only stupid conduct. There are no spiteful children, only spiteful acts. There are no selfish children, only selfish actions.

They don't know any better and it is your job to teach them, educate them, help them, encourage them. You start off on the wrong foot if you start off believing they are bad. You're almost bound to fail if you believe them to be faulty. You can't change a bad child but you can change bad behaviour. If you believe the child is good, you're on to a winner immediately. All you've got to do is change the behaviour and that is an attainable goal.

It is awfully detrimental to say to a child, 'You are a bad child'. It sets something up in their mind that is hard to shift. Better to say, 'You've done a naughty thing', or 'You've been naughty'. This they can do something about. But if you tell them they are bad, there is nothing they can do about that and it affects them.

> ## YOU CAN'T CHANGE A BAD CHILD BUT YOU CAN CHANGE BAD BEHAVIOUR

Be up around people you love

Your job from now on, as a Rules Player, is to be up around people you love. No more moaning. No more complaining. No more grumbling. These things will no more issue from your lips. You are, from now on, the positive one, the perpetually cheerful, 'always up' one, around whom good things revolve and happen.

When asked how are you, instead of saying, 'Can't complain, mustn't grumble', in future you will say, 'Fine, good, marvellous'. No matter how crummy you feel, no matter what sort of a day you've had, no matter how low, down or fed up you are. And do you know, the interesting thing is that when you do say 'Marvellous', even if you don't feel it, you'll find something positive to say to follow it up with. Whereas if you'd said 'Been better', then the follow-up thoughts would be all negative. Try it – honestly, it really works.

In future, right from today, from this very second, you have to become the one who is always jolly, up, cheerful. Why? Because someone has to, or everybody will want to end it all. This life is hard and treacherous. Someone has to lift the burden, lift the spirits, lift the gloom. So who's it going to be? You, that's who.

I know, I know. You'll be sitting there reading this, thinking, 'Why me? Why lay this burden on me?' Because you can do it, that's why. But do it secretly (remember Rule 1), without fuss or bother. Just a simple change of heart, change of direction. From now on you cannot be anything but up around those you love. OK, moan to strangers. But loved ones get the full treatment. Up, up and away.

SOMEONE HAS TO LIFT THE BURDEN, LIFT THE SPIRITS, LIFT THE GLOOM

Successful people, those who have got it licked, are invariably cheerful. They care more about what people around them are going through, feeling, suffering than their own petty problems. They invariably want to know what's wrong with you rather than moaning about their day. They think positively, act positively, project confidence, verve and enthusiasm.

I had a friend who went to live abroad in a country where he spoke very little of the language. But he said his mood lifted whenever he was there because he didn't know the words for fed up or miserable or down. When someone asked him how he was, he could only say 'Happy', because that was the only word he knew to reply with. He found that when he said it, he felt it.

Give your kids responsibilities

Children grow up and leave home. They go from helpless babies to mature adults who have sex and drink beer while your back is turned. The secret is to try and keep pace with them. As they grow you have to back off more and let them do more. You have to resist the urge to do everything for them and let them fry eggs* or paint dustbins** for themselves.

It's a delicate balancing act. You can't give them more responsibility than they can handle, but at the same time you can't hold them back. And when you do let them fry eggs or paint dustbins for the first time, they are going to make a mess – yolk on the cooker, paint on the garage floor. It's the mess that most often makes a parent say, 'No, you can't'. But we have to break a few eggs (ha ha) to be able to fry one. We have to gloop a bit of paint if kids are going to be able to carry out any DIY job for themselves when they are grown up.

When they are tiny and learning to drink from a cup for the first time we expect spillage. We stand there with kitchen roll in our hand prepared to mop up. But by the time they are teenagers

---

* This one comes from my own son who, when he was asked what being a grown-up meant, said it was being able to fry eggs as he wasn't allowed to – he was about eight at the time. I felt so mean I got him cooking breakfast every day for a month until he was sick of frying eggs.

** This came from a friend who was always angry with his father. When I asked him about his relationship, he complained that as a kid he was never allowed to do anything to help. He finally lost it with his father when his father was painting a dustbin and the kid wanted to help and his father said no. But why? It wouldn't have hurt. Why the father was painting a dustbin in the first place remains a mystery.

we've forgotten the art of hiding the kitchen roll behind our back waiting for them to spill stuff. We expect them to be able to keep their room tidy first time. But they've never done it before. They don't know how to do it. They have to learn and part of that learning process is doing it badly, doing it differently from how we, as adults, would do it. Our job is to help them. To hand them responsibility slowly, bit by bit, but with guidance.

We expect them to do everything right first time, no spillage, no broken eggs, no paint on the floor. It is our expectations that are unrealistic. Growing up is a messy business.

> # AS THEY GROW YOU HAVE TO BACK OFF MORE AND LET THEM DO MORE

Your children need to fall out with you to leave home

They've never tidied their room. They've played their music long and loud and driven you mad. The two of you are about at breaking point and you wonder where you went wrong as a parent of a sullen, moody, dressed-in-black teenager. They are monosyllabic, depressed (but miraculously cheer up when their mates come round), always hungry, rude, mercenary, trouble-some and relentlessly embarrassed by you. And you blame yourself. It is all your fault. You have somehow failed them. Rubbish. This is all good stuff.

Look, your kids have got to fall out with you to be able to leave home. If they loved you too much they couldn't leave. You've nurtured them, wiped their bums, dressed them, fed them, doled out money for all of their lives. And they don't want to feel grateful. They want to leave, to drink too much, have sex and use grown-up swear words. They don't want to be your dar-ling little angel any more. They want to be spiky and daring and rude and adult. They want to discover and explore and get into trouble all by themselves. They need to break the chains, rip the parental ropes off and run over the hill shouting that they are free at last. How on earth can they do that if they are still in awe of you, still feeling so attached to you, still loving you so much? They have to break free by *not* getting on with you before they can come home again as something more than just your child.

It is all natural and you should welcome it and be glad to see the back of them. Chuck 'em out early I say and then they'll be back all the sooner. You can't ruffle their hair ever again or tuck them in or read them a story, but you will find a grown-up friend comes back and you can share a whole new relationship with them.

> # THEY HAVE TO BREAK FREE BEFORE THEY CAN COME HOME AGAIN AS SOMETHING MORE THAN JUST YOUR CHILD

Hold them back and they'll resent you for longer. Take it personally and they'll take longer to return because they'll feel guilty.

And you can show this to your teenager: Don't give your parents too hard a time. They are feeling just as threatened by this new relationship as you are. Give them a break; they're making it up as they go along, just as much as you are.

RULE 84

Your kids will have friends you don't like

'Oh no, not Mickey Brown – again!' This was my mother's cry, every Saturday morning. She hated Mickey Brown. Loathed and detested him with a vengeance. Why? I have no idea. She disliked most of my friends but she saved up all the venom for poor Mickey Brown, whom she took against before she ever met him.

Look, your children will sometimes have friends you don't approve of. It's natural. Live with it. As kids we are attracted to other kids who are different from us. It's our way of finding out. We go for the very poor kid or the very rich kid because we have no experience of it and want to know what it is like. We go for the ruffian or the spoilt princess or the kid from a different ethnic background to ours or the ragged urchin who smells or the autistic kid or the one from the council estate or the smug middle-class one whose parents are accountants.

Whatever it is, we will be tempted to disapprove. It's human nature, but we mustn't. We must be supportive, encouraging, welcoming and open. Why? Because if our child is hanging out with other kids that test our tolerance, it's a good thing. It shows we are bringing them up not to be prejudiced or judgemental. And if they aren't being prejudiced or judgemental, neither should we be.

The funny thing is that Mickey Brown's parents couldn't stand me either. He wasn't allowed to play with guns and I was always smuggling them into his house when his parents weren't looking. I didn't like guns particularly – and we are talking cap guns here – but I did love getting him into trouble . . .

IF OUR CHILD IS HANGING OUT WITH OTHER KIDS THAT TEST OUR TOLERANCE, IT'S A GOOD THING

One of my own children had a birthday party and insisted on inviting a kid in his class who had serious adjustment problems (what we used to call a 'naughty child' but you can't do that any more – see Rule 80). When his parents came to collect him they were quite tearful, as it was the first birthday party this poor kid had ever been invited to. What's that? His behaviour? Oh he was a little angel and didn't put a foot wrong. In your dreams. He behaved true to type and I was heard muttering, 'Never again, he never comes here again', for many weeks afterwards. No, seriously he played up a bit and wrecked the place, but no more than any of the others did. One of the others, a supposedly good kid, was caught filling one of my wellington boots with cheese sandwiches and jelly – second hand if you get my drift.

Your role as a child

So, you're a grown-up now and probably don't recognize yourself as a child. But you are still a child, although you'll get strange looks if you park in a 'parent and child' space if you happen to go shopping with your mother or father.

Until both of your parents have passed on and you have been promoted, so to speak, you remain a child. And you have a responsibility. You have a duty – now you are a Rules Player – to be courteous, thoughtful, patient and co-operative towards your parents.

Yes, yes, I know they drive you mad but from now on you have a role and it is simply this:

- To behave impeccably with them.

- To look after them if that's what they want/need.

- To back off if that's what they want/need.

- To listen to them when they witter on, without losing your rag or sighing.

- To appreciate that they have had a long and hard life and gathered a lot of experience – some of which may be of some use to you – and you won't know if you carry on shaking your head and ignoring everything they say.

- To visit, write, phone, communicate more often than you think you should – but probably not as much as they think you should.

- Not to bad-mouth them in front of your children but to talk them up as being the greatest grandparents in the world.

- To be pleased when they come to stay and happily let them watch whatever TV programme they want without complaining.

And why will you do all this? Because they gave you life, brought you up. Yes, yes, I know they made mistakes along the way but you forgive them all of them (see Rule 76) and you turned out fine. Oh yes you did.

Parents deserve decent treatment when they get old and need attention and someone to listen to them and take them seriously – and they make great baby/dog sitters (and usually free as well).

> # YOU HAVE A DUTY
> # TO BE COURTEOUS,
> # THOUGHTFUL AND
> # CO-OPERATIVE TOWARDS
> # YOUR PARENTS

Your role as a parent

Gosh, this is a tough one. You have a role and it is important, but how do we define it, make it real for you, so that you can live by it, put it into practice?

Steve Biddulph, who wrote *Raising Boys** and other books about parenting, said in a recent newspaper interview that our job, as parents, is to keep our children alive until they are old enough to get help for themselves . . .

If you are crazy enough to take on the role of parent, then you are signing an invisible contract with your children to give and get them the very best of everything you can. And I don't necessarily mean material possessions. Your mission, should you choose to accept it, is to be all that the very best parenting requires. You will be encouraging, supportive, kind, patient, educational, loyal, honest, caring and loving.

You will have to make sure they eat the best food for developing children. You will supply them with the best education for their talents and skills. You will aim to develop their interests in all areas and not just the ones you are keen on. You will set clear boundaries so they know what's what, and what they can and can't do – and with clear and acceptable levels of discipline should they overstep the mark. You will adjust your degree of supervision to match their age – little ones need closer supervision than big ones. You will always provide a safe haven for them to come home to – no matter how much trouble they've got themselves into in the big bad world outside.

You will be firm, loving, sharing, caring and responsible. You will set them standards and be a role model to them. You won't do or say anything you wouldn't be proud of them knowing.

---

* *Raising Boys: Why Boys are Different – and How to Help Them Become Happy and Well-balanced Men* by Steve Biddulph (Thorsons, 2003; 1st edn Finch, 1997).

You will stand up for them, protect them and keep them safe. You will stretch their imaginations and feed them with stimuli so they grow up creative, excited about the world and raring to go.

You will approve of them, boost their self-esteem, improve their confidence and send them out into the world literate, educated, polite, helpful and productive members of society. And when the time comes for them to leave the nest, you will help them pack and keep giving that support while they find their feet (or should that be wings?).

Not much then, really.

> **YOUR MISSION, SHOULD YOU CHOOSE TO ACCEPT IT, IS TO BE ALL THAT THE VERY BEST PARENTING REQUIRES**

SOCIAL RULES

Every day we come into contact with real live human beings – at work, commuting, in shops, out and about – people we might have met before or often complete strangers. The world is full of people with whom we interact. Those interactions, small or large, can be life-affirming or deeply unpleasant. So, what follows are a few social Rules. These aren't set in stone. They aren't a revelation. They are a reminder.

We will look at some Rules for dealing with people at work. After all, that's where we spend an awful lot of our time and anything we can do to make our career more successful and our working life happier, more satisfying and productive, and most of all enjoyable, surely can't be a bad thing?

Social Rules are the fourth circle we draw around ourselves (the first is self, second is partner, the third is family and friends, the fourth is social relationships). It's terribly easy to see our own group, social class, or any level of community as the right one, the important one, the better-than-yours one. But each community sees itself as that. How much better to draw that fourth circle around ourselves so that it includes people from other backgrounds, other ethnicities, other communities, so that we feel part of the big community, the human one. It is better to include more than to exclude even one. And it is very easy to exclude for whatever reason, to assume that it is a 'them' and 'us' situation, when actually we are all 'them', we are all 'us'.

We have to treat everyone with respect or what's it all about? We have to care about everyone or the whole thing falls apart. We have to help each other no matter who they are, because if we don't there won't be anyone to help us when we need it. We have to be the first to put our hand out. Why? Because we are Rules Players.

We're all closer than you think

I have a friend. Not a good friend particularly, more of an acquaintance. He's a regular sort of a chap. Runs a computer business. Has a family. Normal, regular, 9 to 5, straight, nothing unusual about him. Or so he thought.

He is English, born and bred. He used to have a bit of a rant about immigration. Went on a bit about numbers but you always felt it was a bit deeper than that. He found out not long back that he was actually adopted. Nothing wrong with that – plenty are – but it set him to tracing his family. Yep, you've guessed it. His father was a foreigner.* Now you wouldn't know it to look at the man but he's only half as English as he thought he was. Interesting.

If you trace back anyone's history it's going to throw up a lot of different bits from different communities and ethnic group-ings. None of us is in any way 'pure'. The whole thing has been melted, shaken and stirred and blended until any one of us would be hard-pressed to swear where we originated. Go back far enough and we all contain something a bit different. Apparently, half of all Europeans carry a line that can be traced back to Genghis Khan – and he came from Mongolia.

My point? Don't judge others, because we are all human, all drawn from the same melting pot. We are all related if you go back far enough. There is no difference. We have to accept other communities, other cultures even if they are very different from ours because the difference between us is so very little when you wipe away the veneer we all wear.

---

* That's his word, by the way, not mine.

Yes, we may wear different clothes and speak different languages and have different customs but we all fall in love, all want someone to hold and hug, to have a family, to be happy and successful, not to be afraid of the dark, to live a long time, die a good death, to be attractive and not to get fat, old or sick. What does it matter if we wear a suit, a sari or a grass skirt if deep down we all cry when we are hurt, laugh when we are joyful and our stomachs rumble when we are hungry? The veneer can be wiped away in a second and then we are all the same, all quite lovely and quite, quite human.

THE DIFFERENCE BETWEEN US IS SO VERY LITTLE WHEN YOU WIPE AWAY THE VENEER WE ALL WEAR

RULE 88

It doesn't hurt to forgive

It's easy to be angry. It's easy to get riled up and mutter or to make rude gestures and swear. It isn't so easy to be forgiving. And I'm not talking about turning the other cheek here or any of that stuff. I'm talking about seeing it from the other person's point of view. And being forgiving.

I had an incident recently on holiday which basically involved a very wet cyclist mouthing off because he decided someone (no, it wasn't me) had driven too close to him and nearly forced him into a ditch. He was loud, rude, aggressive, out of order and foul-mouthed. I tried to speak to him reasonably on behalf of the person he was being abusive to and he gave me a mouthful as well. Then he rode off and shook his fist at me which made his bicycle wobble and inside I laughed, a lot. I found it easy to forgive him not in any religious sense but because I could see he had chosen the wrong holiday.

He had obviously been persuaded that the cycling holiday would be fun but it was in hilly, really hilly, countryside, and it had rained all that day. He was tired, wet, aching and very unhappy. How could I not forgive him? If I had foolishly chosen that holiday, I too would have been grumpy, ready for a fight, fed up, tetchy and raw. I felt quite sorry for him and could sense a great deal of his unhappiness. Yes, he was in the wrong to use such foul language – especially in front of children. Yes, he was ready for a fight and intimidating and aggressive. But he was also me or you or anyone else in that situation, cold, wet, miserable. And who is to say we wouldn't have lost our temper if we too had chosen the wrong holiday?

Being forgiving doesn't mean we have to be pushed around or put up with nonsense. We can stand our ground and say, 'Sorry I don't need to take that', but we can also make an attempt to forgive because we can see it from the other person's point of view. Maybe the word is tolerant rather than forgiving. But either way we don't have to mistake forgiveness or tolerance or whatever with meekness. We can still be saying, 'Shove off with your bad language and sad bicycle and your mother smells of hamsters', while feeling sorry for the poor idiot at the same time. He was a good man who did a naughty thing.

Just bear in mind that anyone you come into contact with who hacks you off may have had a really bad time before they got to you.

> **BEING FORGIVING DOESN'T MEAN WE HAVE TO BE PUSHED AROUND**

It doesn't hurt to be helpful

We said in the previous Rule that the angry person you encounter may have had a bad day before they got to you. Let's try to make it a good day for all of them before they get to someone else. Let's spread a bit of goodwill around out there and then maybe, just maybe, mad cyclists won't be quite so ready to rear up and be abusive and aggressive. Perhaps no one had been kind to him that day. Perhaps no one had been kind to him for a very long time. See, it's all your fault. If only you'd been a bit nicer to him, he wouldn't have taken out his wet angst on the rest of us that day.

Always offering a hand and being generally decent to everybody is really easy once we get into the mindset that it's what we are supposed to be doing. It can become your 'default' behaviour. So your first reaction becomes 'Yes, sure, I can show you how to do that, no problem', rather than 'I'm very busy, can't you ask someone else?'

Try it as a different approach at work and see what it does for your reputation and career. Getting known as someone who is always ready to help does not get you known as a pushover. Quite the reverse in fact.

If you see someone in trouble – even if it's only that they've spilt their shopping getting it into the back of the car – you can always go up and say, 'Can I help?' If they want you to they'll accept and if not . . . well, you tried and that's the main thing.

This is all about going into every day thinking the best of people, being the first to smile, seeing where somebody might need a hand instead of bustling on past. It's about trying to see a situation from their viewpoint, being sympathetic if they have problems – you don't have to solve them all. It means taking the time and trouble to make sure people around you are OK. And yes, this does mean strangers as well. If we all took the trouble to smile occasionally at strangers, the world might start each day on a slightly less confrontational footing.

> THIS IS ALL ABOUT GOING
> INTO EVERY DAY THINKING
> THE BEST OF PEOPLE

What's in it for them?

We all want to win. At work and in most aspects of life, winning is good, and we don't like to lose. No one sets out to be a loser. But we do tend to think that if we are going to win then someone else, someone around us, has to lose. But it doesn't have to be that way.

In every situation, the smart Rules Player weighs up the circumstances and asks: 'What's in it for them?' If you know what's motivating the other person, you can help steer the situation (and your actions) so you get what you want, but they feel they've got something out of it too. The 'win-win' mentality might have come out of the workplace, but it applies to pretty much every situation and relationship.

To work out what others are likely to want and need, take a step back and remain a little detached, so you're looking at the situation as if from outside. Suddenly it stops being *you* and *them*, and you'll stop thinking that *they* need to give way in order for *you* to win.

> ## YOU GET WHAT YOU WANT, BUT THEY FEEL THEY'VE GOT SOMETHING OUT OF IT TOO

Dealing with somebody who's got the hang of this Rule is a rewarding experience – people will look forward to working with you, because there's an air of co-operation and understanding. Once you've learned to always look for the other person's 'bottom line' you'll become very fluid in your negotiations and will gain a reputation for being adult and supportive – and that's another bit of winning for you as well.

And it's not just in workplace negotiations that this win-win reaps rewards. Try it at home too. If you're debating where to go on holiday, and you desperately want to go horse riding in France, think 'What's in it for them?' – what is it about that holiday that will make *them* happy? Highlight those aspects and they're more likely to agree. If you're struggling to think of anything that will appeal to them, you need to think more broadly – maybe you can find a place where you go horse riding while they go fishing or sailing. You see how it works. Just asking the question 'What's in it for them?' helps you think it through.

Being a parent is another area where this works. If you just lay down the law without considering what your children want and need, they'll rebel, or at least be difficult to handle. But again ask 'What's in it for them?' and you'll see the situation from their perspective and handle it better. Winner.

Hang out with positive people

If you want to be successful in your life, at work, socializing, you need to be aware that there are two groups of people to hang out with. First, there are those who lift you up, are positive about life, have energy and enthusiasm, walk their walk, talk their talk and generally make you feel great to be alive. And then there are the moaners, who bring you down to their level of inactivity. The second group are not the group to hang out with if you want to make things happen and be happy.

So hang out with the positive, smart people. I mean people who feel life is an exciting challenge worth wrestling to the ground and having fun with. The sort of people who have interesting points of view, who make you feel good talking to them, who have positive things to say or suggest rather than moaning. The sort of people who tell you that you look fantastic rather than criticize you.

Earlier on we talked about clearing clutter out of your life – physical stuff (see Rule 46). Now maybe it is time to clear some people clutter (hmm that sounds terribly LA).* Let's have a look at the people you do hang out with.

Which ones can you honestly say make you:

- feel enthusiastic about seeing them?

- make you rise to every challenge?

- make you laugh and smile and feel great about yourself?

- support you and nurture you and encourage you?

---

* If this book is on sale in LA then I meant somewhere else entirely.

- stimulate you with new ideas, new concepts and new directions?

And which ones make you:

- feel depressed after you've seen them?

- make you feel angry, dejected or criticized?

- squash your ideas and pour cold water on your plans?

- don't take you seriously?

- don't make you feel as if you can achieve anything?

Hang out with the first group. Cull the second group – unless they are just having a bad day (and we all have those). Move on, get it done. Ah, but you'll say it is cruel to prune friends ruthlessly like that. Well, I suppose it is, but then I want to enjoy my friends not moan about them. If I find myself doing that, I prune them. No point hanging out with people who don't make you feel good – not unless you like being down.

> **NO POINT HANGING OUT WITH PEOPLE WHO DON'T MAKE YOU FEEL GOOD**

RULE 92

Be generous with your time and information

As you get older – and probably not any wiser (see Rule 2) – you will learn a lot of stuff. Some of that stuff will be important to other people, often younger people, but not always. Share what you know with them. Don't hold on to information for the sake of it. Don't hold on to your time for the sake of it. What would you be doing with it that could be in any way more worthwhile?

If you have a special talent or skill, pass it on. I don't necessarily mean you have to spend all your spare evenings down at the local youth club teaching young tearaways all about whatever it is you do or know about.

But if the opportunity arises then go for it. I was recently asked to give a talk to a bunch of six-year-olds about what it means to be an author. At first I thought: 'But I'm not an author; I might just qualify, and only just, as a writer.' But an author sounded far too grand, too fiction, too grown-up for me. What on earth could I tell six-year-olds about what I do for a living? But, remembering my own Rule, I warmly and graciously accepted and went along. I must say I had one of the most pleasurable mornings in a long time. They were fantastic. They asked brilliant questions, paid attention, chatted in a very adult way, were keen and interested and in general well-behaved and marvellous. It would have been so easy to say no. And you never know what you might inspire in others, what flame you might fan, what encouragement you might give without even knowing.

This Rule especially applies at work. It's very easy to fall into the mindset that if you know stuff that nobody else does, then you have the upper hand. To believe that knowledge is power and you should hang on to every little bit of it. Actually, the most successful people in life are always looking to pass on what they know, to bring on others in their wake. Because if you don't, then who's going to replace you? You make yourself indispensable and you have just wedged yourself in a career rut.

If you're not passing on your talents and skills, what are you doing with them? What great secrets have you got that demand to be withheld from the world? Or is it laziness? Successful Rules Players say yes as often as possible because there is an incredible experience to be had in passing stuff on. And it is genuinely useful. Don't go thinking that what you know is of no use to anyone. I guarantee it will be quite the opposite because the second you say yes, you become one step up from all those that say no. That makes you important, successful, decisive and generous. And that makes you special.

IF YOU HAVE A SPECIAL TALENT OR SKILL, PASS IT ON

Get involved

Get involved in what? Anything really (or at least almost anything). I guess what I mean by this is to take an interest in your world. Don't watch it on television but go out there and interact with it. Too many people are living their lives through the lives of others seen on that little screen. Or even living their life vicariously through the lives of others in the real world (gossip and tittle-tattle keeps them going). There is a great big wide world out there full of life, vitality, energy, experience, drive, excitement. Get involved means get out there and be part of it. Get out there and find out what it all means and how it works. Watching TV is warm and safe and comfortable. Being out there can be scary, cold, uncomfortable. But at least you know you're alive.

People are always complaining that life goes faster as we get older. But my experience is that the more we do out in the world, the more time seems to be stretched. If we watch TV, whole evenings can vanish before our very eyes.

Getting involved means co-operating, contributing, taking part. Not watching from the sidelines while someone else has your life for you. Getting involved means rolling up your sleeves and getting your hands dirty but having an experience along the way, a real experience. Getting involved means joining in, offering help, volunteering, turning a theoretical interest into a real one, being out there and talking to people. Getting involved means having fun, real fun, not TV fun. Getting involved means helping other people appreciate and enjoy their lives a bit more than they would have done without you.

I have noticed that successful people – and that is what this book is all about, and by successful I do mean content and happy rather than wealthy or famous – have outside interests that don't earn them any money or bring them any kudos. Stuff they do for the fun of it, to be helpful, to encourage others.

They often find the time by doing it instead of watching more TV (seriously).

They become volunteers, mentors, school governors, local business advisers, charity workers. They join groups, associations, clubs, societies. They get out there and belong and have fun. They put themselves out there to make a difference or share an interest. They go to evening classes in ridiculous subjects. Maybe they laugh and poke gentle fun at themselves for doing it. Maybe they even sometimes wish they hadn't got involved as some things can creep up and take over your life. But they are part of something. Part of the world – in a full and proper sense.

> **GETTING INVOLVED MEANS ROLLING UP YOUR SLEEVES AND GETTING YOUR HANDS DIRTY BUT HAVING A REAL EXPERIENCE ALONG THE WAY**

Keep the moral high ground

Boy is this a simple one to say and a really difficult one to live up to. I do appreciate that it's a tough one, but I know you can do it. It takes a simple shift of vision, from being the sort of person who acts in a certain way to being a different sort of person who acts in a different sort of way. Look, no matter how rough it gets you are never going to:

- take revenge

- act badly

- be very, very angry

- hurt anyone

- act without thinking

- act rashly

- be aggressive.

That's it, the bottom line. You are going to maintain the moral high ground at all times. You are going to behave honestly, decently, kindly, forgivingly, nicely (whatever that means), no matter what the provocation. No matter what the challenge thrown at you. No matter how unfairly they behave. No matter how badly they behave. You will not retaliate in like kind. You will carry on being good and civilized and morally irreproachable. Your manners will be impeccable. Your language moderated and dignified. There is nothing they can do or say that will make you deviate from this line.

Yes, I know it's difficult at times. I know when the rest of the world are behaving appallingly, and you have to carry on taking it on the chin without giving in to your desire to floor them with a savage word, it's really, really tough. When people are being horrid to you it's natural to want to get your own back and lash out. Don't. Once this rough time has passed, you will be so proud of yourself for keeping the moral high ground that it will taste a thousand times better than revenge ever would.

I know revenge is tempting, but you won't go there. Not now, not ever. Why? Because if you do you'll be sinking to their level, you'll be at one with the beasts instead of the angels (see Rule 9), because it demeans you and cheapens you, because you will regret it and lastly because if you do, then you're no Rules Player. Revenge is for losers. Taking and keeping the moral high ground is the only way to be. It doesn't mean you're a pushover or a wimp. It just means that any action you do take will be honest and dignified and clean.

> ## KEEPING THE MORAL HIGH GROUND WILL TASTE A THOUSAND TIMES BETTER THAN REVENGE EVER WOULD

RULE 95

Just because you have, doesn't mean they have to

I was at school with a guy whose family had relatively little money when he was growing up. Actually, compared to many people in the world, he really wasn't that badly off. But compared to most of the other kids in school he had less. This is partly what drove him to get a high-powered City job eventually, and he is now very comfortably off. Probably better off than most of the people he was at school with. But boy does he have a chip on his shoulder about money. He hugely resents anyone having money they haven't worked as hard for as he has, and makes cutting remarks to friends, such as, 'It's nice that you can afford to go to the Bahamas for a month on holiday. Not everyone can, you know'. That's certainly true, but he can.

Look, everyone has their own troubles to cope with, now and in the past. You can't give other people a hard time just because they haven't suffered like you have. Whether you had a rotten childhood, or are poor, or have a relationship that doesn't make you happy, or didn't get the job you wanted, or can't have a dog because you're allergic – whether your troubles are big or small, the point is that it's not *their* fault. You have no idea what else your friends have had to contend with in their lives, or will do in the future. They may not have it any easier than you on balance.

If you go round trying to make your friends feel guilty about having some things easy or good, you'll just end up damaging your friendships. Then are you going to go round resenting people with more friends than you? No, I know you wouldn't do that – but some would. And what's the alternative? Would you wish a miserable childhood or poverty or a bad marriage or redundancy or a dog hair allergy on your friends? I certainly hope not. If you're living your life the best you can, you'll want to see as many other people happy as possible. So you should be pleased every time you encounter someone who didn't have it rough.

I don't want to be unsympathetic to people with tough lives. Of course I'm not. But by becoming bitter you make your life even worse. Just be happy for other people if they don't have the crosses to bear that you did or do.

That friend of mine, by the way, he may have been born into a relatively poor family, but he was born with brains. That's how come he got into Oxford University and a plum City job. But does he feel guilty about all those people who weren't born as clever as him? Of course he doesn't. But I bet there are people with chips on their shoulders about the fact that he went to a top uni and they didn't. Gosh, what a lot of wasted resentment there is in the world. Let's do our bit by not adding to it.

> ## BY BECOMING BITTER
> ## YOU MAKE YOUR LIFE
> ## EVEN WORSE

Do compare yourself with other people

This isn't the original version of this book, you know.* In the first edition (as in this one) I invited readers to contact me with their own Rules. This particular one – which I couldn't agree with more – was suggested to me by a 16-year-old schoolboy from India. I mention this for two reasons. Firstly, because it just goes to show that you're never too young to follow the Rules. And secondly, because I think it's significant that this comes from someone who is still in education and therefore expects to learn from other people. It's a Rule that demands a measure of humility that all of us could do with (well, alright then, I could do with).

People often tell us not to compare ourselves with others. The argument for this is that it's arrogant if we think we're better, and demoralizing if we think we're worse. Also that we're all different so the comparison can't be accurate. However, when you're at work, you're constantly set targets for performance, and quite right too. And in fact we should set our own targets in our personal lives (see Rule 29). And this applies not only to our plans, but also to our own behaviour and development.

None of us is perfect – we all know that. We all wish we could be more patient or kinder or more tolerant or harder working or better parents or more sensible with money. But how much more? The best way to decide what to aim for is to use someone you respect as a touchstone. 'I'd like to be as well organized as this person' or 'as calm as that person'. You see? You're comparing yourself to other people, but in a positive way. It means you can see how much work you have to do, and you can see that

---

* Don't worry, you're not missing out. This version is bigger and better.

it's achievable. You don't have to tell them you're using them as your guide, although you can certainly ask their advice if it would help.

You might think that it could be depressing always to be comparing yourself with people who are better than you. But as my 16-year-old friend wisely points out, one person is good and the other is better. No one is scoring badly here, and anyway you get extra brownie points for the fact that you're being honest with yourself about where there's room for improvement, and then taking positive steps to achieve this.

Seeing the people around us as teachers is something that comes naturally when you're 16. Sadly we can lose that attitude as we get older. But if we have any sense we surround ourselves with good, positive people, so actually it would be odd if we couldn't learn from them, wouldn't it? And it's our best chance of beating Rule 2.*

> YOU CAN SEE HOW MUCH
> WORK YOU HAVE TO DO,
> AND YOU CAN SEE THAT
> IT'S ACHIEVABLE

---

* You mean you haven't learnt them by heart? Rule 2 is 'You'll get older but not necessarily wiser'.

Have a plan for your career

So where are you going at work? Have you a plan? A goal? Even a humble aim? If you don't have any of these, chances are you're going to drift. If you do have a plan, you stand a better chance of getting to where you want to be. Knowing where you want to be is 90 per cent of the battle. Knowing where you want to be means you've sat down and thought about things, that you've been conscious about your future and have focused your attention on it.

Once you've looked ahead and decided where you want to be – and there is no right or wrong about where that is, you can be as determined and ambitious as you want – you can plan the logical steps you need to get you there. And once you have those steps, you can work out what you need to do to make each a reality. Is it further qualifications? Experience? To change jobs? To change the way you work? Whatever it takes for you to make those steps is what you have to do. Don't stagnate. Don't get stuck in a rut.

We all need to work to earn a crust. Staying at home watching daytime TV really isn't an option. Work keeps your mind fit and active as well as getting you in touch with other people, and work also presents a daily challenge. Believe you me, we are better off with it than without it.

If you don't have a plan you could end up anywhere. Yes, sure that might be exciting but I doubt that many people end up happy and successful merely by chance. It's something you have to work at, consciously. And having a plan is part of that conscious effort. I know luck plays a crucial part in some people's lives, but only a very few. And formulating a plan and working hard while you're waiting for the luck to turn up doesn't mean that it won't, or that when it does you aren't free to throw away the plan completely.

If you're not busy planning and working towards the next goal, there is a real chance you can fall into a downward spiral of despondency and apathy. Successful people have 'get up and go' – and when they don't have it naturally, they artificially create it. They pretend to if you like, but the very act of pretending gets them up and about. Try it, it works.

> ## STAYING AT HOME
> ## WATCHING DAYTIME TV
> ## REALLY ISN'T AN OPTION

Look at the long-term ramifications of what you do for a living

It is no longer safe or responsible or ethical to carry on working without thinking about what we do and the effect it has. I'm not going to question you about what it is you do. That is entirely for you to do. As a writer, I am aware that a lot of good trees could die young because of me. Balanced against that are the positive effects (I hope) of what I write, and people who are employed as a result of the writing. Ah, but I have no control over their working conditions so I'm off the hook there. Or am I?

> AS A WRITER I AM AWARE
> THAT A LOT OF GOOD
> TREES COULD DIE YOUNG
> BECAUSE OF ME

So, for me it is dead trees, the electricity I use in my office and the pollution caused by trucks delivering books to book stores, to name but a few by-products of my sitting here tapping away. What about you? Handled any hazardous waste lately? Or designed a missile guidance system? Or logged an entire rain forest? Or does your work provide an essential service or product; does it make people happier, wealthier or more successful?

What we do for a living has an impact. We can be working in an industry that pollutes, causes harm, is unpleasant and bad. Or we might be working to help others, to benefit people positively. Knowing that what we do causes an effect – for good or bad – doesn't mean we have to instantly chuck everything up and change jobs. Nor does it mean we can sit back and relax and think we're doing OK just because we work in a caring job.

Every job, every industry has some ramifications – good and bad. Everything we do at work can have great benefit or cause harm. We have to weigh it all up and check how we feel about it. And if we are unhappy we can leave, but not too fast because there's a great chance we can change things from the inside.

I worked in one industry for a while where I was aware that things were a bit dodgy, so I adopted the line of asking, 'What if the press get hold of this, what would that do to us?' I wasn't whistle-blowing or opposing anyone, merely asking. But it did draw attention to the fact that what was happening was slightly the other side of a fine line. Maybe you could do the same. Or maybe you can slowly, quietly, use the influence that you have and the actions you are able to take, to change things ever so slightly for the better.

RULE 99

Be good at your job

How we behave at work has an effect on our colleagues. We need to have standards – and stick to them. We have to be moral and decent and honest and trustworthy, of course. But here are a few other tips to help you become fantastically successful along the way.

- Treat your job as important and do it to the very best of your ability. Don't stand still but learn all the time; stay ahead of your industry and new developments. Put in extra hours if you must but don't be seen to be too hard-working – a laid-back approach gains you more respect.

- Always be on the look-out for ways to improve the lot of everyone rather than just yourself. Think in terms of 'we' rather than 'I'. You are a part of a team and should fit in and be a part effectively and efficiently.

- Try to spread a little happiness as you go. Don't badmouth people. Stick up for the underdog. Compliment people and be genuine about it. Don't indulge in gossip or tittle-tattle. Keep your own counsel and be a bit aloof. It'll get you promoted.

- Dress smartly and try to make a good impression. Maintain high standards and put in the hours. Try not to go to work to sleep or steal the pens or look for love. You are there to work, so get on with it.

- Try to be kind to colleagues – they are as lost as you once were. Give them a break, a chance, a bit of slack. Encourage them by example. Be a role model for junior members of staff. Try to understand your boss's point of view and to see things from the company perspective.

- Understand the politics of office life – and don't get involved of course – but use it to your own advantage. Don't be frightened to put yourself forward or to volunteer (just so long as you know what you are volunteering for). There is no kudos in being work-shy. Be proud of being effective and efficient.

- Know your boundaries. Know how to say no, and mean it. Don't let anyone take advantage of your good nature. Be assertive without being aggressive.

- Enjoy what you do. Have a passion for your work. Have fun.

> # WE HAVE TO BE MORAL AND DECENT AND HONEST AND TRUSTWORTHY

RULE 100

Be aware of the damage you are doing

This Rule doesn't mean, as yet, that you have to do anything. All it means is a conscious decision to evaluate what you are doing to the environment, the world, and whether it is a good thing or a bad thing. You might choose to change what you do in the light of this evaluation. Or you may not, either because you figure what the heck or because you figure you're pretty 'green' already and don't need to change anything.

The reason I say 'Don't do anything as yet' is that it is all too easy to rush headlong into action without having all the facts in front of you. You need to know if the changes you are making are actually making things better or worse. For example, when my youngest child was born I was seriously concerned about the reports of the damage disposable nappies are doing. Apparently they take some 500 years to decompose. But I was also concerned that terry nappies take a lot of washing with all the usage of electricity, soap, water etc. And some argue they are both as bad as each other when it comes to damaging the environment. Trouble is, you have to use something or you risk damaging your carpets . . .

So you might like to consider what car you drive; what sort of heating you use in your house; how you get to your holiday destinations (planes aren't that environmentally friendly by all accounts); whether you recycle; if somebody else can use what you don't want – that sort of thing. I leave the details entirely up to you (heaven forbid that I should lecture anyone on these matters) but it's good to have a conscience about these things and to try and minimize the damage we are doing.

This goes back to the big theme underpinning all the Rules, namely that we need to go through our lives with our eyes open, conscious and aware of what we are doing and the effect we are having on the environment and on other people around us. We don't have to become goody-goodies but we should at least be giving it some thought.

I think the time for complacency is over and it really is time to consider the impact we make quite carefully. And once we have considered it, we might like to start making a few changes to improve things. If we all did a little bit, it would make a grand difference.

WE DON'T HAVE TO BECOME GOODY-GOODIES BUT WE SHOULD AT LEAST BE GIVING IT SOME THOUGHT

Be for the glory, not the degradation

We can work for the glory of humankind or we can try to bring it all crashing down into degradation. Shakespeare is for the glory, a crack house is for the degradation. A village fête on a warm summer's afternoon is for the glory, stealing someone's purse is for the degradation. And it doesn't have to be tame; a parachute jump for charity is for the glory, porn is for the degradation – but an erotic movie can be for the glory. Get the idea?

Anything that makes us more than we are, makes us strive for perfection, improves us, challenges us, excites us in a good way, makes us rise above our base nature and brings us out into the sunshine is for the glory.

So what are you going to be for? The glory or the degradation? Well, for the glory of course. My fear is that you will think this is all about being good and that has a bad press. All our lives we have been told that being good is a bad thing, somehow dull, for the meek and namby-pamby, the sandal wearers, the holier-than-thou brigade. Being good hasn't had a lot going for it. As a kid at school if you tried to be good you got beaten up. At work if you try to be good they call you the boss's pet.

Well, being good, being for the glory is a private thing. You don't have to tell a soul. If you keep it quiet you are being good. If you brag about it you are a goody-goody. If you interfere with others and try to make them be good, you are a do-gooder. Just make a decision to be for the glory and say nothing.

JUST MAKE A DECISION

TO BE FOR THE GLORY

AND SAY NOTHING

Be part of the solution, not the problem

This goes further than just being good, being for glory not degradation. This is about positive, affirmative action. Look, if we don't take some action then this world, this fabulous planet of ours, is going to hell in a handcart. I was reading an article the other day about Easter Island and how it could stand as a perfect metaphor for our own sad predicament.

> IF WE DON'T TAKE SOME
> ACTION THEN THIS WORLD,
> THIS FABULOUS PLANET OF
> OURS, IS GOING TO HELL IN
> A HANDCART

Easter Island was settled by a Polynesian race around 800 years ago.* They found an island heavy with wildlife and heavily wooded with trees. Within a few short years they had eaten their way through the wildlife and chopped down all the trees. They also polluted the rivers and were on the verge of extinction. The only thing that has rescued them is tourism.

---

* Don't write in if I got the facts vaguely wrong – it's a metaphor.

Planet Earth has no tourists. There is nothing going to rescue us so they can take our photo. We all have to start being a part of the solution now, and stop adding to the mayhem, the destruction, the problem. And we start to be part of the solution when we stand up and get counted. We stop the problem when we stop saying, 'I was just doing my duty', or 'It was part of my job'. Come on, we have to stop the nonsense now or we're going to be relegated to being some vast amusement park for aliens – who aren't coming.

So the Rule is to start looking for ways we can personally contribute to the solution. We have to take part, get involved, find solutions, take action, get off our backsides and contribute. If you want your life to feel right, to be good, to be successful and mean something, you have to put something back. You have to pay back your loan. You have to reinvest in life and that means caring and wanting things to get better.

Check what history would say about you

So what is history going to say about you? What do you feel in your heart of hearts is going to be your epitaph after you've gone? And I don't mean what is engraved on your tombstone but written in some great cosmic record of the universe. Personally, I don't think I'll even warrant a footnote. But if I do, I would like history to record that I had a go, made an effort, tried my best to make a difference. That I stood up for what I believed in, stood up to get counted and stood up for my rights. I would like history to say, maybe, that I got up off my backside and just stood up – it would be enough.

And you, my friend, what would you like? What do you *think* history will say? What would you *like* history to say? Is there a gap between these two? Can you bridge it? What do you have to do to make that gap connect? Think about both what it would say about you as a person, and about your deeds.

We have to care, if we want to be successful, that those who come after are going to inherit a better world than the one we found ourselves in. You remember all those books on self-sufficiency that were all the rage back in the 1970s?* Well, a key thing they all seemed to have in common was they said if you had land, you had to make better use of it than the person who had it before you. You had to improve it. Same with this world. We have to consciously make the effort to improve it before we go. We have to take responsibility for what we've been given and make a better use of it before we shuffle off and pass it on.

---

* Yes, yes, I too was sold the dream and moved to the country to grow my own yoghurt, wear sandals and eat lentils. It didn't last long, not for me anyway.

How will we point at the polluted oceans, the dried-up rivers, the melted ice caps and say to our metaphorical children, 'One day all this will be yours – oh and sorry about what we did with it'? I think they may be a little angry at us. History may indeed write us off as termite people. We have destroyed and polluted and slaughtered and made a pretty poor show of things. Individually we can make a difference. We must make a difference. Individually history must hold us accountable.

The trouble is there are so many people who won't change because they think they won't be held accountable. If there is no one watching, they think they can get away with murder. History will make short work of them.

> # HISTORY MAY INDEED
> # WRITE US OFF AS
> # TERMITE PEOPLE

Not everything can be green

I've just heard about a chap who has invented shoes that recharge your mobile phone battery while you're walking.* Brilliant. I want a pair but they all look like rugged walking boots – designed for areas where recharging equipment isn't available, such as jungles and deserts. I'll have a pair when they make them in Oxford brogues. Not everything can be green. Not everyone can be as organic and as green as we would have them be.

OK, we've gone through the rant about the state of the world and what we're doing to it. Now I'm going to give you a tiny get-out clause. Not everything can be green. There have to be by-products. There has to be some pollution. There has to be some damage. We are vast in number – billions of humans living on the planet have to have an effect – and we have to live.

> ## NOT EVERYONE CAN BE AS ORGANIC AND AS GREEN AS WE WOULD HAVE THEM BE

---

* Trevor Bayliss – he also invented the wind-up radio.

There will always be some damage. Our job is to limit it, but it is unrealistic to attempt to eliminate it altogether. It's all a question of balance, of priorities.

It is unrealistic to demand the immediate elimination of all motor vehicles in the world; it's not going to happen. But we can do our bit by buying cars that use less fuel, emit cleaner exhaust fumes, use recyclable materials in their construction. But they won't be totally green, they can't be.

We might all rush off to disaster zones to lend a hand but we'll fly there and aircraft emit huge quantities of exhaust fumes. You see, we are making choices all the time. Driving to work, heating our homes, what we wear, what we eat. We can't expect everyone to be as green as we want to be. We can't expect everything to be as green as we would have it.

If we all manage to achieve a reduction it helps. If we all do our bit it helps. If we are all conscious about what we are doing it helps. But we can't expect perfection. We can't turn things around overnight. If you're trying so hard to be green that it's causing you a great deal of stress and your life is suffering as a result (just try to go food/household shopping and buy nothing at all in plastic and you'll quickly see what I mean), then stop. Make an effort but accept that it's never going to be totally perfect. Just so long as we are trying to do something, it helps.

Put something back

I firmly believe that none of us asked to be born and that this world doesn't owe us a living, or anything. But by the same token we are in hock up to our armpits. Sure, we didn't get a choice about being here, but once we *are* here we get fed and watered, entertained and amused, challenged and educated, awed and flabbergasted. It's all here on offer for us. We can do pretty much anything we want. We can take from this world all it has to offer. And this world has an amazing amount to offer to all of us.

We can take and take and take. There is nothing to say we can't. What I am suggesting is that we sleep better at night if we put something back. After the show be one of the volunteers clearing up.

Be generous with everything. Be generous with your generosity. You don't have to give money but rather your time and care. If you have a special talent, use it to help others in some way. If you have facilities, lend them to others who need them. If you have the power to effect change for the better, then use it. If you have influence, use it.

> **WE SLEEP BETTER**
> **AT NIGHT IF WE PUT**
> **SOMETHING BACK**

And if you don't? I'm sure that we all can make a difference in our own small way. We might have to look carefully or use our imagination a bit or be creative in how we define 'giving something back'.

We don't all have to become charity workers or missionaries but we could sponsor a child in need. We don't have to turn our house into a shelter for the homeless but we could start a wildlife patch in our garden. We don't have to become totally organic but we could recycle a bit more or just ask questions about the companies we choose to buy from.

I guess we all have to ask ourselves: 'Is this world a richer place for me being in it? Will I leave it a better place than when I came into it? Have I made a difference to someone's life? Have I put something back?'

Find a new Rule every day – or occasionally at least

So, with this book you now have 100 or so Rules for a successful and fulfilled life. Phew. But don't think it's over yet. There is no time to sit still, there are no tea breaks for Rules Players. As soon as you think you've got it sussed, you'll fall flat on your face. You have to keep moving forwards. You have to be inventive, creative, imaginative, resourceful, original. This final Rule has to be to keep thinking up new Rules, not to stand still, to carry on developing this theme, adding to, improving on, evolving and growing and changing these Rules. These provide a jumping-off point. They're not a revelation, more a reminder. These Rules are a starting point for you to pick up and run with.

I've tried to avoid the pedestrian ('Time is a great healer') and the humorous ('Never tip anyone who isn't looking') and the impractical ('Love everyone'), the plain daft ('Turn the other cheek' – you get hit twice that way, better to run I say), the wibbly ('Everyone's a rainbow'), the obviously wrong ('There are no victims') and the very, very difficult ('Spend 35 years in a cave and you'll find the secret of the universe' – and get a wet bottom). I've also avoided the trite ('It'll be alright on the night' – my experience is it never is) and the unpleasant ('Don't get mad, get even').

I hope you too will follow a similar plan when you formulate new Rules for yourself. I guess the main thing is that you need to continually formulate your own Rules. When you learn something – from observation or just an illuminating moment – then absorb the lesson and see if there's a Rule there for future use.

Try to find a new Rule every day – or at least occasionally. And I am quite genuine about wanting to know what you come up with – if you want to share them. Being a Rules Player is a lot of fun and it is quite fascinating to try and spot other Players. Whatever you do though, don't go telling everyone about it. Keep it secret, keep it safe – but you can tell me at www.facebook.com/richardtemplar

Being a Rules Player requires dedication, hard work, perseverance, keenness, ambition, enthusiasm, devotion and sheer doggedness. Keep at it and you will live a fulfilled, happy and productive life. But go easy on yourself, we all fail from time to time and no one is perfect – I'm most certainly not. Enjoy and have fun and be good.

> # THESE RULES ARE A REMINDER. THEY ARE A STARTING POINT FOR YOU TO PICK UP AND RUN WITH

THE RULES OF HAPPINESS

Happiness is not a permanent state of affairs. It's a transient thing. There will always be bad days, dark times, bleak years even. Understanding this is the first step to greater happiness, in an ironic way, because once you stop expecting to be happy *all* the time, it makes you less unhappy when you aren't happy. If you see what I mean. In any case, without the lows we wouldn't appreciate the highs, and happiness is very much about appreciation.

Now, while you can't avoid the lows, there's plenty you can do to feel happy as often as you can, and for as long as you can. So that your life's graph of highs and lows is weighted as heavily as possible towards the highs.

Happiness is habit forming. The more you can train yourself to feel happy, the easier it will become. And yes, I know to some people that the very idea you need to 'train yourself' to be happy won't sit very well because it makes it sound like an effort, and you might think that you shouldn't have to *try* to be happy. It's something that should just happen – that you're entitled to even. Sorry folks. You will need to put a bit of effort in, but the upsides are so big that surely it's worth it. And the training is much easier than, say, going to the gym – it's just about learning to think differently.

You'll find that most of the Rules we've already covered in *The Rules of Life* relate to happiness in some way, and several of them are especially relevant. However, for this new edition here are ten brand new Rules which are all absolutely central to living a happy life.

Take the long view

Happiness is notoriously hard to define, of course. Are you trying to achieve a constant state of elation, or simply a basic sense of satisfaction with your life – or some point in between? Obviously permanent joy is an unrealistic aim; however, a broad contentment with your lot is a perfectly reasonable thing to want.

Even so, any kind of high level of delight is going to be transient. Joy is not a thing you can hold on to for long, and nor should it be. How boring would it be to be endlessly ecstatic, forever in raptures? It would cease to be delightful because we'd take it for granted. So there have to be bad bits too. The question is, can you be happy when you're having a bad day, or a rough month, or a depressing year?

Of course you can. If we're defining happiness as being content with your life, it would be ridiculous to imagine that even the most satisfying life would be all perfect. If that's what it takes to be happy then no one could ever achieve it, and the whole concept of happiness would be a nonsense. So you have to find a way to maintain your happiness even when things aren't going well.

We know that however bad it gets, it's never so bad if you have people to support you, if you consciously appreciate what you *do* have, if you have some kind of belief system, if you like yourself, if you keep busy, if you do things you enjoy. But on top of that, the key to coping with a bad day – or month, or year – is not to measure your happiness by the standard of now, but by the long term.

So don't ask yourself, 'Am I happy right now?'* Ask yourself, 'Am I happy overall?' or even 'Are there elements of my life I'm happy with?' Look back over the last few years and consider how your life is going in general. And look forward to where you seem to be heading. That way, even though today is something of a downer, you can see the bigger picture and recognize that you are still fundamentally happy. Today is just a bad day in a happy life. Or a bad day on one level but a happy day on another one.

And if you can't? Well, I'd suggest reading this book again and really thinking about Rules that especially resonate with you. What small changes can you make to your life and your outlook? And don't just rely on my observations of people – watch the people you know as well. See who seems happy and think about why they manage to see their lives in such a positive light. We can all achieve happiness if we want it. It might take some effort, but few things in life are more worthwhile.

> # DON'T ASK YOURSELF, 'AM I HAPPY RIGHT NOW?' ASK YOURSELF, 'AM I HAPPY OVERALL?'

---

* Unless you are, of course.

RULE 2

Do something you're good at

It's hard to overstate this one. You'd think it would be obvious, until you see how many people don't follow it. When you do something you know you're good at, that you are totally immersed in, in flows confidence, self-esteem, enjoyment, passion, positivity and all the other things that bring happiness.

Even if you can't find work doing something that excites you, you can still make sure that you do your job well. Even in a tedious-but-it-pays-the-bills kind of a job, there's a world of difference between going through the motions and doing it really well. If you have to be there, for goodness' sake make sure you're the best you can be at the job, if only because you'll be far happier if you do. (Best of all, do that *while* formulating a plan to move on to something else more fulfilling.)

And whether or not you currently have the job you'd choose, what about all the things you do with the rest of your time? Whether it's a hobby, or cooking for the family, or voluntary work, or sport, do something you can lose yourself in, that gives you a real sense of achievement.

Please note that I'm not saying you should never do anything you're *not* good at. Even a concert pianist must once have been not good at the piano. We'd never learn if we couldn't start anything we weren't already good at. And some things have to be done and will never be our forte. In my case, for example, cleaning the house. But be conscious that in order to be happy you need to spend as much time as you reasonably can doing things that you can be proud of.

When you know you're doing a thing well, you get into a rhythm that is really therapeutic. Whether you're wowing an audience with a presentation, swimming like an otter, turning your child's fear to confidence, creating a photograph of the sunset that looks better than the real thing, helping a patient to feel comfortable and relaxed, or baking a cake the family will have devoured before it's even cold, that sense of being lost in something that flows smoothly because you know exactly what you're doing is one of the most beguiling feelings there is. For many of us, it's when we're at our happiest. So obviously the more we can find that feeling, the more often we'll be happy. And since happiness is largely a matter of habit, we'll get into the habit of feeling good about ourselves more and more.

> # WHEN YOU KNOW YOU'RE DOING A THING WELL, YOU GET INTO A RHYTHM THAT IS REALLY THERAPEUTIC

RULE 3

Like yourself

One of the Rules is that you need to accept yourself (see Rule 4). But if you want to be truly happy you have to go one better. Yep, you have to actually like yourself.

Some of us have no problem with this, in which case you can skip on to the next Rule. But most of us struggle with it at least sometimes. To begin with, you have to *want* to like yourself. It's no good feeling that you shouldn't like yourself, that this would make you vain or arrogant or self-centred. It can be a tough call, but you have to break down any psychological, religious, cultural or self-creating feeling that you don't deserve to like yourself.

Listen, this isn't about thinking you're a fabulous person without any faults. It's about being relaxed in your own company and appreciating your qualities. I don't know about you, but I like lots of people who are flawed, tricky, complicated, imperfect. So I don't see why I shouldn't be allowed to like myself too, with all my shortcomings. Why should we be harder on ourselves than we are on everyone else?

So recognize that while you're not perfect, you're no worse than lots of likeable people. And the same Rule applies to other people. I have friends and family who – despite the fact that I like them – occasionally behave in ways that I'd prefer them not to. I can see past that and still like them. So it stands to reason that I too can be likeable even when, sometimes, I do something I later regret.

This is particularly hard for people who haven't been lucky enough to grow up loved and valued. If this is you, I know this might not be easy. However, I really want you to grasp this because you of all people deserve it, and happiness may elude you until you do.

Start by finding bits of yourself to like. Make a conscious note of them (you don't have to tell anyone else). Be aware of the times you can look back at a particular incident and think, 'I like the way I handled that'. Now build on that, focus on the qualities you're comfortable with, and keep looking for aspects of yourself you enjoy. If someone could wave a magic wand and change any part of you, which bits would you choose to hang on to? Those are a good place to start in cataloguing the things you like about yourself. And really listen if people commend you for something, or give you a compliment, instead of just brushing it off. Once you get into the habit of noticing your positive attributes instead of focusing on your shortcomings, you might well be surprised how many of them there are.

THIS ISN'T ABOUT THINKING YOU'RE A FABULOUS PERSON WITHOUT ANY FAULTS

Look from the other direction

A friend's teenage son, who is quite competitive, had a swimming match recently. When I asked him how the main race had gone he replied, 'I did really well. I came third, but I would have come second if I hadn't messed up the start'. This delighted me, because he needn't have taken such a positive stance. As far as he was concerned, he might as well have come second so he felt almost as proud as if he had. He could have said, 'It was terrible, I only came third, because I messed up the start. I should have done better'. Lots of people would have seen it that way. But for whatever reason – call it teenage bravado if you like – he chose to look at it from the other direction.

And the result of his approach? He was happy with the result – which is what we're interested in here – when exactly the same result could have made him unhappy. It was all about his perception. If you can learn to recognize when you have a choice about how you respond, you can do this too. Did you fail to get a promotion (miserable), or did you come really close (happy)? Have you arrived home drained and aching after an exhausting day (grumpy), or is it lovely to put your feet up with a cup of tea in your own chair and not have to move until bedtime (mmmm . . .)?

But a leopard can't change its spots, right? Some of us are programmed to look on the bright side while others are made to see the dark side. Well, this is only partly true. Yes, some lucky people seem to be born looking at life from the happy direction, but if you can get into the habit of recognizing when there are two directions you can see things from, you'll already be less negative than when you think there's no other perspective. Try it. Go on. Next time you're tempted to feel sorry for yourself, look for a different angle.

This is a great example of how habit-forming happiness is. The more you do it, the easier it becomes. And the more you can recognize that other angle, the easier it gets to adopt it yourself. Of course there'll be times you can't shake off your disappointment or sadness, but they'll be less frequent and it will take more to upset you. And that's got to be worth it. After all, can you imagine how great it must feel to be happy about coming third in a race?

NEXT TIME YOU'RE
TEMPTED TO FEEL SORRY
FOR YOURSELF, LOOK FOR
A DIFFERENT ANGLE

Spin it

We're such gullible creatures really. If you tell us anything enough times, we'll start believing it. So why not use this to your advantage? If you keep telling yourself you're happy, you will be happy. Try it, if you don't believe me.

It takes a little while to build up of course. And if you tell yourself you're happy 10 times a day, and then tell yourself 20 times a day how miserable you are, guess which one will win. But if you're serious about it, yes, it will work.

Think about it. Imagine the toughest parts of the world to live. The favelas of Rio, the deserts of Sub-Saharan Africa, the Delhi slums, Siberia, the sink estates closer to home – do you think you'd be happy living there? No. And yet, do you think everyone there is miserable? No, they're not. Of course some of them are, and with good reason, but there are always people who can smile and find enjoyment in any kind of life. Sure, their expectations may be lower than yours (which I think gives you something to be happy about), but it's more than that. They choose to believe they're happy. You see, happiness is just a belief, and you can indeed choose it.

You can also think about what makes you happy, and arrange for more of it to happen: being with people you love, keeping busy, doing something you're good at, helping other people, eating chocolate.* That's what those people with tougher lives than you or me do, and if it can work for them, it can work for us.

Here's a trick I've learnt. I do this every night, and it's almost like a meditation in the sense of how good it makes me feel. Before I go to sleep, I run through the day and recall all the

---

* I wouldn't be doing my job properly if I didn't advise you to be moderate about this one.

good bits. I resolutely ignore anything negative, however large a part it played in my day. I simply remember everything positive, from the big stuff down to a friendly checkout person or a nice hot coffee after coming in from the cold.

You can do this in your head, or it can help to tell it to someone – even someone who isn't actually there but who you'd like to be with. There's something extra convincing about the objectivity you get when you relate it to someone else. It's hard to find a better way of ending the day, and waking up happy the next morning.

> ## HAPPINESS IS JUST A BELIEF, AND YOU CAN CHOOSE IT

Mix it

One of the best things about a bad day at work – or school or college or anywhere else – is being able to go home at the end of the day and shut the door on it. Block out the horrid world and hide away in your own sanctuary until you're ready to pop your head out again.

So what happens when things aren't going well at home? Obviously you need to escape into work – or school or college or whatever – and lie low there until it feels safe to go back inside. There's nothing wrong with running away, you know. Of course some kinds of running away aren't a good idea, but on a temporary, small scale it's very underrated, and often it solves the problem. All it needed was a bit of time or space. When you get home the family is less grumpy or the heating's been fixed or just taking the time out has given you a shift in perspective.

Longer-term and more serious problems are helped by having somewhere else to go too. If your boss constantly belittles you, at least you can feel confident at home. If one of your family is ill and a constant worry, at least when you're at work you can feel in control.

This gives us the next Rule. It's important to move in more than one world, so that you have the best chance of retaining some part of your life that makes you happy even when other parts are going through a phase that is worrying, draining, upsetting, confidence-sapping, frustrating. Don't be immersed all the time in work, or in kids, or in college or anything else. Make sure you have places you can escape to when you need it: family, work, friends, hobbies.

A life of variety is a lifeline in bad times, but it's also the most interesting and fulfilling kind of life. You can choose your own balance – obviously you can choose what you like, it's your life – so that you get all the good bits. It's not just about having an escape. Different circles bring you different ingredients for happiness. You might get all the love and confidence you need from staying at home with the kids (or you might not – I don't know), but it may not help you feel respected, for example. Another part of your life might supply mental stimulation, and another excitement, or relaxation. Sometimes you can get a lot of what you need from one area of life, but to get everything you need to make you happy, along with an escape when things go badly, you really need to mix it up a bit.

> # DON'T BE IMMERSED ALL THE TIME IN WORK, OR IN KIDS, OR IN COLLEGE OR ANYTHING ELSE

RULE 7

Find a distraction

One of my close friends really struggles to be happy. He's a worrier by nature. He almost always has something negative in his life to worry about (don't we all?), and if there isn't anything obvious he seems to create worries. It's just the way he's made. He worries about things that might never even happen. What if his wife's illness turns out to be more serious than it seems? What if the company decides to make redundancies and he's in the firing line? What if interest rates rise and he can't afford the mortgage?

But he doesn't have to settle for a life of constant worry. Remember how habit-forming happiness is, along with thought patterns. If you can change your thoughts, you'll change your mood. Change them for long enough, and you'll change your prevailing mood. The good news is that, if you're persistent, there are lots of ways to change your thought patterns. I'm going to give you a couple of suggestions, and you can take it from there.

First of all, it's great to have some kind of occupation that you can't worry through. It might be sport, gardening, playing with the kids, building model trains, reading, work, baking, tracing your family tree, organizing your stamp collection, you name it. Anything that works for you. If there are times you're especially prone to think negative thoughts – on the train to work, say – find a distraction that suits. Do crosswords, knit, plan work in a notebook. The only proviso here is not to pick something potentially addictive to you, such as drinking or computer games or gambling. This isn't the time to create a new problem.

There will still be times when you worry or dwell on miserable thoughts and you don't have a ready distraction. So you need to find a thinking-only solution. The critical thing here is to catch yourself thinking negatively, and say to yourself, 'Ha! Got you. Stop it at once!' Then you need to offer your mind an alternative train of thought or it will go back to its old ways. How about having a 'happy thought' you use in these circumstances, that you just switch into? For example, the plot of the novel you're writing in your head, a daydream about scoring the winning goal, planning the design of the house you want to build as soon as you have the money, working out the intricacies of a new computer game you'd like to invent, planning a knockout report for your boss that will get you instant promotion . . . you get the idea.

Finally, you may find it helps to consider the upside of whatever is worrying you. This doesn't work for all things, but suppose you're worried about being made redundant. Why not think about all the opportunities this will give you, and all the plus sides to it? The irritating colleagues you'll never have to see again, the long commute you can give up, the chance to start your own business or change careers or move out of the city? Once you learn the art of self-distraction, you'll find it much easier to deal with less-than-happy thoughts.

> # IF YOU CAN CHANGE YOUR THOUGHTS, YOU'LL CHANGE YOUR MOOD

RULE 8

Know who you value

One of the absolute basics of happiness is security. It's impossible to feel really happy if you don't feel safe. And that doesn't just apply to physical safety but also emotional security. What you want is a good, solid support network so you know that if things go wrong in life you have somewhere to turn, someone who will catch you if you fall.

You might have different people for different areas of your life: colleagues at work you can trust, mentors whose advice you can ask and whose wisdom you can call on, friends who you can count on to be there, family who would do anything for you, parents who will always give you a roof over your head.

Know who these people are. And if you don't feel confident that you can rely on the support you have in some areas, work on building relationships that will give you what you need. It's far easier to cope with backstabbers and fair-weather friends at work if you have even just one colleague you know you can absolutely trust. A strong relationship with your partner, your parents or your siblings will get you through even the worst trauma. So make sure you know who's on your side.

They say 'count your blessings'. Well count your friends too. Be conscious and aware of who these people are that make up your safety net, appreciate them even when you don't need them, and let them know you value their love and friendship. Why? Because apart from the warm feeling it gives them, it will reinforce your own sense of security and that will feed into your happiness levels.

Oh, and I hope it goes without saying that you need to give these people everything you expect from them, should they be the ones going through it. If they call on you, being there for them will give you a sense of worth that will add to your long-term happiness even in the most unhappy of circumstances.

A STRONG RELATIONSHIP
WITH YOUR PARTNER,
YOUR PARENTS OR YOUR
SIBLINGS WILL GET YOU
THROUGH EVEN THE
WORST TRAUMA

Break down the blocks

What's getting in the way of your happiness? What are the barriers that are preventing you from being satisfied with your lot? Difficult relationships? Not enough money? A tedious job? Nope – that was a trick, hope you didn't fall for it. None of these things are stopping you from being happy. You should know by now that all the barriers to happiness are inside you. Yes, that's right, it's all coming from you. We've already looked at some examples, such as worrying and thinking negatively. What are your own personal blocks, the things about you that hold you back?

If anyone asked you what needs to change to make you happy, the answer is not your job or your relationship or your past. And I'll tell you why: because if you change all these things, you still haven't changed your outlook on life. You'll still be the same person, waiting for some happiness to drift past close enough to grab it for a moment. Whereas if you change your outlook, none of these things – job, relationship, lifestyle – *need* to change because you can create your own happiness wherever you happen to be.

I'm not saying you can't change your job or move house or whatever if you want to. If you don't like the present situation I thoroughly recommend doing what you can to change it. Just don't expect it to make you happy. At best you may find yourself a bit less unhappy.

Yes, yes, I know it's not easy. Indeed it can take a lifetime. Mind you, that's not a lifetime of being miserable with a sudden flash of happiness at the end. That's a lifetime of becoming progressively happier. Surveys show that people generally get happier as they get older – at least until the last few years. I always used to think, when I was young, that this was weird because the older you are the less life you have left. However, as I get older myself, I realize that this isn't the important thing – it's just an outside factor, like the job or the relationship. The thing is that as you get older you simply get better at the things that make people happy – the things inside you. You become more confident, more self-assured, you learn to value yourself, you build strong relationships around you. Of course not everyone manages to do these things, but most people do, and you will because you're a Rules Player and you'll persevere until you get there.

> **YOU SHOULD KNOW**
> **BY NOW THAT ALL THE**
> **BARRIERS TO HAPPINESS**
> **ARE INSIDE YOU**

Take control

Do you feel in control of your life? Do you think that fate determines the path we follow, or do you consider it's down to you to make your own choices? I have no more idea than anyone else which is actually the case, but I can tell you that people who believe that they have control over their lives tend to be happier than those who don't.

If you already feel in control, that's great. If you don't, however, it's an important thing to work on. Many things in life are indeed out of our control. You can't determine when your car breaks down,* or whether one of your close family gets seriously ill. You may feel powerless about having to work for an impossible boss. You can't determine the weather.

Then again, as they say, 'There's no such thing as bad weather. There's just the wrong clothes'. Even the most random external events aren't completely out of your control, because you can choose how you react to them. What will you do about the car – sell it and buy something more reliable, or take a chance on it? How can you support the person who is ill? Are you going to stay in the job or hand in your notice?

The more free choices you can make, the better you'll cope with whatever life throws at you. Actually, sticking with the status quo – keeping the car, staying in the job – is a choice, but it doesn't always feel like it. It's easy to feel saddled with a situation you don't like.

So always be conscious that you have a choice. Sometimes the alternative is worse than what you have now, but you're still making a choice to put up with things. If you keep the job you'll be happier for knowing that you *could* leave but you've chosen to stay. OK, you're not as happy as you'd feel if the boss

---

* Why would you ever choose that?

left and was replaced by a new dream boss. But a lot happier than if you feel you have no control. You do have control, you're wielding control, you have the power – and you're using it. Apply this control to every corner of your life. You may choose not to change very much, but there's always an alternative, however bleak, and you're not being carried along relentlessly on a path you wouldn't choose. You *are* choosing your path, every day.

> # THERE'S ALWAYS
> # AN ALTERNATIVE,
> # HOWEVER BLEAK

HAD

ENOUGH

YET....?

Hey, it's not only life you know. If you're smart, you'll want to learn how the most successful people behave at whatever it is: life, money, work, relationships, kids. Luckily I've done the hard work for you – the years of observing, the distilling and sieving and summarizing what really makes a difference into handy little Rules.

I've always been anxious not to stretch the Rules principle too far, but following huge demand from readers I have tackled those big important areas that affect us all. So in the pages that follow you'll find a 'one Rule' taster of each of the other Rules books:

Rules of Wealth
Rules of Work
Rules of Management
Rules of Parenting
Rules of Love

See what you think. And if you like them, there are plenty more in each of the books.

Anybody can be wealthy – you just need to apply yourself

The lovely thing about money is that it really doesn't discriminate. It doesn't care what colour or race you are, what class you are, what your parents did, or even who you *think* you are. Each and every day starts with a clean slate so that no matter what you did yesterday, today begins anew and you have the same rights and opportunities as everyone else to take as much as you want. The only thing that can hold you back is yourself and your own money myths.

> **YOU HAVE THE SAME RIGHTS AND OPPORTUNITIES AS EVERYONE ELSE TO TAKE AS MUCH AS YOU WANT**

Of the wealth of the world each has as much as they take. What else could make sense? There is no way money can know who is handling it, what their qualifications are, what ambitions they have or what class they belong to. Money has no ears or eyes or senses. It is inert, inanimate, impassive. It hasn't a clue. It is there to be used and spent, saved and invested, fought over, seduced with and worked for. It has no discriminatory apparatus so it can't judge whether you are 'worthy' or not.

I have watched a lot of extremely wealthy people and the one thing they all have in common is that they have nothing in common – apart from all being Rules Players of course. The wealthy are a diverse band of people – the least likely can be loaded. They vary from the genteel to the uncouth, the savvy to the plain stupid, the deserving to the undeserving. But each and every one of them has stepped up and said, 'Yes please, I want some of that'. And the poor are the ones saying, 'No thank you, not for me, I am not worthy. I am not deserving enough. I couldn't. I mustn't. I shouldn't'.

That's what this book is about, challenging your perceptions of money and the wealthy. We all assume the poor are poor because of circumstances, their background, their upbringing, their nurture. But if you have the means to buy a book such as this and live in comparative security and comfort in the world then you too have the power to be wealthy. It may be hard. It may be tough but it is doable. And that is Rule 1 – anyone can be wealthy, you just need to apply yourself. All the other Rules are about that application.

Get your work noticed

It's all too easy for your work to get overlooked in the busy hurly burly of office life. You're slaving away and it can be hard to remember that you need to put in some effort to boost your individual status and personal kudos for your work. But it's important. You have to make your mark so you stand out and your promotional potential will be realized.

The best way to do this is to step outside the normal working routine. If you have to process so many widgets each day – and so does everyone else – then processing more won't do you that much good. But if you submit a report to your boss of how everyone could process more widgets then you'll get noticed. The unsolicited report is a brilliant way to stand out from the crowd. It shows you're thinking on your feet and using your initiative. But it mustn't be used too often. If you subject your boss to a barrage of unsolicited reports, you'll get noticed but in completely the wrong way. You have to stick to certain rules:

- Only submit a report occasionally.

- Make really sure that your report will actually work – that it will do good or provide benefits.

- Make sure your name is prominently displayed.

- Make sure the report will be seen not only by your boss, but by their boss as well.

- Remember it doesn't have to be a report – it can be an article in the company newsletter.

Of course, the very best way to get your work noticed is to be very, very good at your job. And the best way to be good at your job is to be totally dedicated to doing the job and ignoring all the rest. There is a vast amount of politics, gossip, gamesmanship, time wasting and socializing that goes on in the name of work. It isn't work. Keep your eye on the ball and you'll already be playing with a vast advantage over your colleagues. The Rules Player stays focused. Keep your mind on the task at hand – being very good at your job – and don't get distracted.

THE UNSOLICITED REPORT IS A BRILLIANT WAY TO STAND OUT FROM THE CROWD

Get them emotionally involved

You manage people. People who are paid to do a job. But if it is 'just a job' to them, you'll never get their best. If they come to work looking to clock in and clock off and do as little as they can get away with in between, then you're doomed to failure, my friend. On the other hand, if they come to work looking to enjoy themselves, looking to be stretched, challenged, inspired and to get involved, then you are in with a big chance of getting the very best out of them. Trouble is, the jump from drudge to super team is entirely down to you. It is you that has to inspire them, lead them, motivate them, challenge them, get them emotionally involved.

That's OK. You like a challenge yourself, don't you? The good news is that getting a team emotionally involved is easy. All you have to do is make them care about what they are doing. And that's easy too. You have to get them to see the relevance of what they are doing, how it makes an impact on people's lives, how they provide the needs of other human beings, how they can reach out and touch people by what they do at work. Get them convinced – because it is true of course – that what they do makes a difference, that it contributes to society in some way rather than just lines the owner's or shareholder's pockets, or ensures that the chief executive gets a big fat pay cheque.

And yes. I know it's easier to show how they contribute if you manage nurses rather than an advertising sales team, but if you think about it, then you can find value in any role and instil pride in those who do whatever job it is. Prove it? OK. Well, those who sell advertising space are helping other companies, some of which may be very small, reach their markets. They are alerting potential customers to things they may have wanted for a long time and may really need. They are keeping the newspaper or magazine afloat as it relies on ad sales income, and that magazine or newspaper delivers information and/or gives pleasure to the people who buy it (otherwise they wouldn't, would they?).

Get them to care because that's an easy thing to do. Look, this is a given. Everyone deep down wants to be valued and to be useful. The cynics will say this is nonsense, but it is true, deep down true. All you have to do is reach down far enough and you will find care, feeling, concern, responsibility and involvement. Drag all that stuff up and they'll follow you forever and not even realize why.

Oh, just make sure that you've convinced yourself first before you try this out on your team. Do you believe that what you do makes a positive difference? If you're not sure, reach down, deep down, and find a way of caring . . .

> # GET THEM CONVINCED – BECAUSE IT IS TRUE OF COURSE – THAT WHAT THEY DO MAKES A DIFFERENCE

Relax

So who are the best parents you know? The ones who have a seemingly instinctive ability to say and do the things that will result in happy, confident, well-balanced children? Have you ever wondered what makes them so good at it? Now think about the ones you privately don't think are much cop. Why not?

All the best parents I know have one key thing in common. They're relaxed about it. And all the worst ones are hung up on something. Maybe they're not stressed out about how good they are as parents (perhaps they should be) but they're hung up about something that affects their ability to be a really good parent.

I know a couple of parents who are neurotically clean and tidy. Their children have to take their shoes off at the door or the whole world falls apart. Even if the shoes are clean. They get really uptight if their children leave anything out of place or make any kind of a mess (even if it gets cleared up later). It makes it impossible for the kids just to relax and enjoy themselves, in case they get grass stains on their trousers, or knock over the ketchup bottle.

I have another friend who is so obsessively competitive that his children are under huge pressure to win every friendly game they ever play. And one who frets excessively every time her child grazes his knees. I bet you can think of plenty of similar examples among people you know.

The really good parents I've encountered, on the other hand, expect their children to be noisy, messy, bouncy, squabbly, whingy and covered in mud. They take it all in their stride. They know they've got 18 years to turn these small creatures into respectable grown-ups, and they pace themselves. No rush to get them acting like adults – they'll get there in good time.

Between you and me, this Rule gets easier with time, though some people still never master it the way true Rules parents do. It's much harder to relax fully with your first baby than with your last teenager to leave home. With babies, you need to focus on the essentials – a healthy baby that isn't too hungry or too uncomfortable – and don't sweat the rest of it. It doesn't matter if their poppers are done up wrong, or you didn't find time to bath them today, or you've gone away for the weekend without anything for them to sleep in (yes, I have a friend who has done this, and no, she didn't sweat it, being a Rules parent).

Much better altogether if you can get to the end of each day, put your feet up with a glass of wine or a G&T,* and say cheerfully to each other, 'What the hell . . . they're all still alive so we must have got something right'.

REALLY GOOD PARENTS EXPECT THEIR CHILDREN TO BE NOISY, MESSY, BOUNCY, SQUABBLY, WHINGY AND COVERED IN MUD

---

* No, I'm not encouraging parents to use alcohol to get them through. Just relax!

Be yourself

Isn't it just so tempting to reinvent yourself when you meet somebody new who you really fancy? Or to try and be who you think they are looking for? You could become really sophisticated, or maybe strong and silent and mysterious. At least you could stop embarrassing yourself by making jokes at inappropriate moments, or being pathetic about coping with problems.

Actually, no you couldn't. At least, you might manage it for an evening or two, or even a month or two, but it's going to be tough keeping it up forever. And if you think this person is the one – you know, the one – then you might be spending the next half century or so with them. Just imagine, 50 years of pretending to be sophisticated, or suppressing your natural sense of humour.

That's not going to happen, is it? And would you really want a lifetime of lurking behind some sham personality you've created? Imagine how that would be, unable ever to let on that this wasn't really you at all, for fear of losing them. And suppose they find out in a few weeks' or months' or years' time, when you finally crack? They're not going to be very impressed, and nor would you be if it was them who turned out to have been acting out of character all along.

I'm not saying you shouldn't try to turn over the occasional new leaf; improve yourself a bit. We should all be doing that all the time, and not only in our love life. Sure, you can try to be a bit more organized, or less negative. Changing your behaviour is all fine and good. This Rule is about changing your basic personality. That won't work, and you'll tie yourself in knots trying to do it convincingly.

So be yourself. Might as well get it all out in the open now. And if that's not who they're looking for, at least you won't get in too deep before they find out. And you know what? Maybe they don't actually like sophisticated. Perhaps strong silent types don't do it for them. Maybe they'll love your upfront sense of humour. Perhaps they want to be with someone who needs a bit of looking after.

You see, if you fake it, you'll attract someone who belongs with a person that isn't you. And how will that help? Somewhere out there is someone who wants exactly the kind of person you are, complete with all the flaws and failings you come with. And I'll tell you something else – they won't even see them as flaws and failings. They'll see them as part of your unique charm. And they'll be right.

MIGHT AS WELL GET IT ALL OUT IN THE OPEN NOW